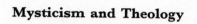

Mysticism and Theology

Mysticism and Theology

An Essay in Christian Metaphysics

by

Illtyd Trethowan
Monk of Downside

Geoffrey Chapman 1975

Geoffrey Chapman Publishers

an imprint of Cassell and Collier Macmillan Publishers Ltd.
35 Red Lion Square, London WC1R 4SG
and at Sydney, Auckland, Toronto, Johannesburg.
An affiliate of Macmillan Inc., New York.

ISBN   0 225 66054 7 (cased)
       0 225 66055 5 (paperback)

Printed in Great Britain by Silver End Press,
Letterpress Division of E. T. Heron & Co Ltd, Essex and London

To Russell Coleburt

Contents

INTRODUCTION

There seems to be no word except "mysticism" to indicate an awareness of God which, although mediated by the finite, is nevertheless
in itself a direct knowledge of him, a contact with him. I shall argue
that such an awareness must be present whenever God is apprehended at all (as opposed to being just taken for granted) and that
Christian apologists must recognise this if they are to make any
considerable impression on the minds of modern unbelievers. The
Christian Revelation is not, in my opinion, philosophically respect-
able on any other terms.

The first six chapters of this book are an attempt to explain that
point of view in the briefest way possible. I am trying to offer a
general outlook on Christianity and, lest the geography of the wood
should be obscured by the trees, I thought it necessary to exercise
the strictest economy, concentrating on what I believe to be those
principles of thought without which Christianity is unintelligible.
There are problems about theism today which an honest man has
to face if he is to accept Christianity. The first three chapters are
concerned with them. The next three consider what seem to me
the chief difficulties for one's thought about the central teachings of
Christianity. This does not mean that I shall be going through a
series of objections to Christianity and offering to refute them one
by one. It means that my account of the general outlook takes note
of certain objections as they arise from it and explains why, in this
context, certain others do not in fact arise.

The conclusions to which these chapters come had been reached
already in two books published in the Muirhead Library of Philosophy (Allen and Unwin): *Absolute Value* (1970) and *The Absolute
and the Atonement* (1971). But in these books, reproducing lectures
given at Brown University, U.S.A., the method adopted was very
different. I found it necessary, for my purposes, to discuss the views
of other writers at length and to reach my conclusions on the basis
of them. The present book avoids all such references to others until
the exposition is complete. I hope that this more straightforward
account, which does not presuppose any specialised knowledge and
is expressed in simple terms, may be of service to a wider class of
readers than the earlier, more elaborate, books. (It is not a collection of extracts from them; the material has been entirely reworked,
and some fresh ground is broken.) In the first three chapters the
reader is only being asked whether this account of the human situation seems to make good sense and whether, if it does, the hypothesis of God can be disregarded. In the West, although it is

possible to be a theist without accepting Christianity, in practice it is Christianity which decides the matter. Thus these chapters together with the three which follow form a single discussion which will be of interest, I hope, to some who would not ordinarily read books about theology.

After that there are three chapters in which I try to emphasise my conclusions by examining in some detail a number of recent books not previously discussed in any book of my own (I have written about some of them in *The Downside Review*). A few short Appendices have the same purpose. The writers in question are referred to in sub-headings, and since other writers are scarcely ever mentioned in the book (and when they are only in an incidental way) an index of names seemed uncalled for. Nor are there any footnotes; those who wish to discover my sources must be referred to the two books above-mentioned. But there is one recent discovery which I must point out here: Ronald H. Nash's *The Light of the Mind* (The University Press of Kentucky, 1969), which I have in view when I speak (on p Qu) of work on Saint Augustine's theory of knowledge.

In the course of writing this book I came across the following sentence in the seventh volume of Karl Rahner's *Theological Investigations* (Darton, Longman and Todd): "the devout Christian of the future will be either a 'mystic', one who has 'experienced' something, or he will not be anything at all" (p 15). Conversion to Christianity carries with it the same requirement: Christian *faith* involves a metaphysical "experience", an apprehension, of God in Christ—that is the central thesis of these chapters. It is one which is opposed to the strongest (or at least the most publicised) currents of theological thinking among us at the moment. But a reaction against them seems to be setting in, and the general attitude of the young to religion suggests that it is going to be intensified. My final chapter concentrates on the relevance of what I have written to the state of affairs with which we are now faced.

K.I.T.

1 HUMAN EXPERIENCE

When anyone mentions his "experience" in the ordinary way he is taken to mean that he has come across something in the past, just as when anyone's "knowledge" is mentioned in the ordinary way we think of information already stored up inside him. But if we are philosophising it is the actual process of coming across things, of getting to know them, with which we are concerned when we raise questions about experience or knowledge.

A fly settles on my nose while I am asleep. There is physical contact, but I am not conscious of it. Then I wake up and become conscious of it—I may not at once recognise it as a fly, but I am aware of something tickling my nose. The fly has now established contact with me in a new way. It is present not just to my body but to my mind. When you come to think of it, this is a mysterious state of affairs. It may not seem so at first sight. For we might be inclined to say that I get a picture of the fly on the retina of my eye, and what is called the mind just reads off the picture. The scientists can explain to us in detail how this is done—messages sent along the nerves to the brain and so forth. But the scientists can explain only what happens on the physical level. When it comes to "reading off" a picture there is an element in the situation which is outside their province. *Consciousness* is something which they cannot explain. It presents itself to us as something which is different from whatever else there may be. And there must be something else for it to be different from.

Some thinkers, indeed, have denied that. All we really have to go on, they have said, is the stream of our consciousness, and we cannot prove that anything is acting upon it—perhaps it produces what we call its objects out of its own resources, making them up somehow as it goes along. Fortunately this sort of "idealism" is out of fashion among us and unlikely to prove an obstacle. But it is perfectly true that we cannot *prove* the existence of objects independent of our own thought. That is to say, if anyone doubts it there is no logical argument which can make him see it. Are we, then, entitled to say that we are *sure* of it ourselves or is it only a well-grounded assumption?

The question which has now been raised is one of fundamental importance. The suggestion that you can never be really sure of anything unless you can produce a cast-iron argument for it is one which I think it most necessary to oppose at the outset. It is surely plain that there is no sense in wanting to *prove* something to yourself if you are already directly in touch with it. I was in touch with that fly. If anyone asked me how I could be sure of it, I could only answer that I was just aware of something affecting my nose and that I can recognise a fly when I see one. Of course, as we shall see in some detail later, I must be careful here. I *could* be making a mistake about seeing something. But there are circumstances in which I *know* that I am not making one. In these circumstances I am directly aware of something as other than myself. If in the same sort of circumstances someone else fails to have this awareness, that should make no difference to me. My own experience is all that I have to rely on. If it tells me unambiguously that there is something there, something *is* there.

We shall have to look more closely at this later on, but I propose to take it as a working principle for the present that we must take our own experience as the final arbiter. This is true all along the line. In following an argument we have to *see* that it works. (It may work, of course, although we fail to see it.) But if we are asked why we are sure that it does we can only answer that we just *see* it somehow. Anyone who doesn't see that, if A=B and B=C, then A=C has to be written off. You can't prove it to him, but you know that you are right and that there is something wrong with him. If we rely on other people's experiences, we are justified in doing so only if we have satisfied ourselves that they are reliable, which means that we must have had a good deal of experience about them.

All this emphasises that consciousness is mysterious; it puts us in touch with *the truth,* and we seem to mean something by that which may not be at all clear. But before pursuing that topic any further we must examine our starting point more closely. It appears that we are directly in touch with a world around us through some operation of our minds as well as physically. We feel that we ought to *explain* this somehow, yet it also appears that it is a sort of basic fact for which we can offer no proof. We may also feel that this whole business of contrasting mind and body with one another is puzzling and perhaps mistaken. Are they really so different? The best way, I think, of dealing with these difficulties is to consider how mind came upon the scene on our planet. This may provide eventually the sort of explanation which we feel to be necessary and show that the difference between mind and body does not cut them off from one another. (They are, manifestly, interdependent.)

Nobody is going to deny that there is a difference between the capacities of human beings and those of the other animals. But nowadays people are often anxious to insist that the difference is only one of degree. This seems strange when you consider the enormous difference between the history of the human race and that of any other animal. The question, however, need not concern us at the moment. If anyone wants to say that mind began not with man but with some other animal it makes no difference in one's account of what its immediate effects must have been. The trouble about this, though, is that we can only guess what "mind" means when it is attributed to other animals. Other animals are said to be "conscious" because they react as we do to situations in which we enjoy consciousness, but no-one can really know what is "going on inside them". I shall suggest later that we can make an intelligible distinction between a life of sensations and a life of thought, but for the moment I propose to consider what happened when consciousness as we experience it made its appearance on the scene, whether or not anyone wants to say that this experience was first enjoyed by other animals.

We may say, it seems to me, that in the first place a body became conscious of itself. This may sound paradoxical, because we think that a body as such is the sort of thing which is *not* conscious and that if consciousness is found in connection with a body it cannot be an activity of the body. But I am not denying that in saying that a body became conscious of itself. It is a way of pointing to the sort of connection between mind and body which seems to exist. Consciousness is a power which comes into existence on the basis of the body—this is part and parcel of the evolutionary view of things which everyone nowadays takes for granted. Our consciousness bears, first and foremost, on the body to which it belongs. It belongs to the body in the sense that it requires the body as its basis. What we are immediately conscious of is our sensations, and these depend on changes in the body. In and through our sensations we are aware of the body undergoing these changes. It is not body simply *as such* that is conscious, but what was once body simply as such is now body with consciousness. And to say that it becomes conscious of itself seems the natural way of describing what has happened.

The difference, however, between body as such and body with consciousness is certainly not just a difference in degree, although attempts are so often made to make out that it is, or that mind and body are not really different from one another at all. People who say this sort of thing are in reaction against those who seem to say that man is a sort of juxtaposition of two distinct entities, mind and body, which live their lives independently of one another. That is clearly untrue. But it is just as absurd to say that mind and body are not different at all. Those who do try to say this are forced, in effect, to deny that the language of consciousness refers to anything *specific,* and although controversy still rages it seems fair to say that this peculiar aberration is being more and more resisted by contemporary thinkers. A human person is plainly a single whole, not two. But, just as plainly, he is a complex whole.

It is necessary to pause at this point to underline the extreme importance of the issue which has just presented itself to us. It can be settled, like all issues of this kind, only by facing our own experience and accepting the assurance which it contains. Our experience, if we attend to it, can assure us that it is *different* from our merely bodily processes, different in a way that strikes us as profoundly significant, although we might not be able to say anything further about this significance. When the activity of consciousness is completely in abeyance—and this certainly happens sometimes, even if we think that it does not happen in sleep—other activities go on, and to say that these activities are of the same *kind* as consciousness seems to make no sense. We may say that all activities have something in common, that they are different kinds of energy, but in the present case the *difference* is all-important. To be just a body is one thing, to be a body with consciousness is very much another, and we have to use a special language for it, that of human persons. Despite all the problems which this raises, vigorously canvassed at the present time, we are still entitled to the essential claim that we are aware of ourselves as living on two planes, interconnected but in themselves radically distinct.

The coming of consciousness, then, means that we are aware of ourselves. *I* come to be. Without consciousness there is no *I*. But "I" means more than bare consciousness. "Bare consciousness" does not really mean anything. Consciousness is always *of* something. And the something on which consciousness first bears, I am suggesting, is the body out of which, so to speak, it has grown. That seems natural. In point of fact that is what we *find* happening. The ground floor of consciousness (again, so to speak) is sensation, our awareness of changes in the body, that is, of the body as it changes. What makes it change? Something impinges upon it, we at once say. But how do we know that? Well, it is obvious that some sort of touching is involved when vibrations strike the ear and we hear something or when light strikes the eye and we see something and so on. Even when it is just a muscular sensation inside you, one bit of you must be pressing on another bit. If any part of the body is left undisturbed there is no feeling of it. This is all true, but again *how* do we know it? The answer must surely be that we are aware of our bodies *as* our own (and parts of our bodies *as* parts of our bodies), and that we are aware of other bodies *as* other because we are aware of them *as* impinging on our own (and aware of parts of our bodies *as* impinging on one another, because aware of them *as* parts of our bodies in conjunction). This is not merely a long-winded way of restating the obvious. The point it makes is that we are aware of other bodies just as *directly* as we are aware of our own, although it is only in their conjunction with our own bodies that we are aware of them. We know that they impinge on us *because we know them in their impinging on us.*

This conclusion, that we are directly aware of things even when we know them only *in* their effects upon us, is one which will affect later conclusions in a big way. So I need to insist on it. We are directly aware of another body as causing our sensations. We *can* make mistakes about this, as about pretty well everything. We can jump to the conclusion that something from outside has hit us when in fact something has happened within our physical organism. But there are occasions when we quite unmistakably "come across" other bodies. The language which we have to use, talking about *our own* bodies, seems of itself to make it clear that we distinguish others from them. The sensations which they cause in us are themselves private to us—a sensation of "green", for example, is what happens to us when objects with a certain kind of surface impinge on our eyes in normal light conditions. If we are wearing tinted glasses we know that the colour we see is due to them. In the same way the colour which we see when we are looking at a distant object is partly due to whatever there may be in the gap through which that object affects us. We can leave it to the scientists to work out the details—the principle should be clear enough. Similarly when we hear a bell our sensations as such exist only in us. The bell communicates with us through vibrations which affect the ear. We are aware of the bell just as something out there which produces *sound* in (and only in) our experience. We may not know just what is causing the vibrations, but we are certainly aware of *something* which is acting upon us to make us hear it. In distinguishing it from ourselves we are *mentally* in touch with it as some other body which we encounter *in* its action on our own body. It is this sort

5

of mental contact which has to be insisted upon as vital for my purposes.

In the second paragraph of this chapter I spoke of "reading off" a picture as a way of describing what happens when we see things and pointed out that one cannot by-pass the fact of consciousness by talk of that kind. Now it may be added that one cannot by-pass the fact of mental *contact,* our direct awareness of bodies not our own, by talk of that kind. It seems natural, perhaps, at first to say that other bodies project a *copy* of themselves on our sense-organs and that they are not themselves in any sense directly in touch with us. The answer to this is commonly accepted by philosophers of all persuasions—it is that if in fact everything which we actually experienced *were* a copy of something we could have no justification for *claiming* that such was indeed the fact. We cannot *know* that a copy is a copy unless we know that it has an original. If everything which is actually in our experience (or before our "minds") were a copy of something the question of its having an original could not arise. For unless we came across originals somehow we could not know that there were *copies* of them. There would indeed be nothing to get an argument started about the possibility that there might be anything at all beyond the sensations which we experience. The suggestion might indeed occur to us, but since there could be no evidence in favour of it we should take no interest in it. So what it amounts to is that our belief in an external world is either a groundless assumption, if we are *really* aware only of our own sensations—which no sensible person is going to accept—or it must be present to our minds *as* external—which no sensible person in fact will want to deny. The point of insisting upon it is that it brings home to us what "being present to the mind" must mean in this context. It must mean a beholding of an object by the mind, for basic awareness of an external world, although it occurs in the medium provided by awareness of our own bodies, is not the result of an inference but is a *union* with that world—a non-physical union.

We are face to face with the fundamental character of human experience. It cannot be described in the proper sense of the word because we cannot compare it with anything else. We are always inside it and can say nothing about situations in which it is not present (we can talk of the external world only in terms of its effects on our experience). When we come across philosophers who fight shy of this notion of awareness or even seem to reject it we cannot offer them a *proof* of it. For this, in my submission, is where we have to start. Although we cannot strictly describe it we can "point to" it, and this may help to bring closer attention to bear on it, making explicit what was only implicit (that I consider to be a philosopher's special business, apart from the clearing up of confusions). To call our awareness of things a *union* is a way of indicating that the knower and the known are brought together with a peculiarly close sort of intimacy in which nevertheless each remains distinct. Our awareness of our own bodies as such (which requires our being aware of them as belonging to a different order from that of awareness itself) is the basic example of it. Our knowledge of other bodies as such (interacting with our own) is another example. This is the special human way of having things *present* to one.

Not only are our own bodies and other bodies present to us together as soon as our human experience begins but we are also present to ourselves as human *persons*. We are aware of ourselves *as* conscious beings and moreover as conscious beings who not only grow in knowledge but also entertain various projects and, in particular, have a keen interest in one another. For the present, however, we shall have to concentrate on *awareness* itself because it is on this that all those activities depend. It is awareness, then, in the first place, that makes us human persons. And it is always a self-awareness. Some people deny this, but it seems to me clearly the case that when we are conscious there is always something going on which has to be called self-awareness even though we are not directly adverting to ourselves. It is surely a truism to say that you can never get away from yourself. *My* experience is always recognised as mine although I am not reflecting on it or talking to myself about it. Awareness is always, so to speak, transparent to itself, and we find ourselves in it. Without going in for introspection or withdrawing attention from what we happen to be doing, we know that *we* are knowing. It is rather embarrassing to have to say something which may seem so obvious, but it is not obvious to everybody.

It is still less obvious to some people that there is a *continuity* of the self. They may feel that if they take up with that kind of notion they may be landed with a "soul" and with the threat of questions about religion which that seems to involve. It is quite true that when once they have acknowledged man's peculiar intellectual or spiritual powers they are on a slippery slope which ends in religious belief. But they can hold themselves up if they want to at several stages on the way. Sometimes the trouble is simply that there is no positive proof of this continuity except that it seems to force itself upon us. That, however, is the best possible evidence for it. In fact we are aware of ourselves, if we face up to it without inhibitions, as the *same* people which we were when we started in some way which we may find it hard to talk about but which we all recognise perfectly well. That is not to say that it is not also as puzzling and mysterious as consciousness itself. But the truth of it is just as plain as that of consciousness. There are indeed "split" personalities. But the apparent exception proves the rule.

This is perhaps the right point at which to look back on the question of the relation between our human awareness and mere sensation, the question, in other words, of what "goes on" in the other animals. For it does seem right, when we look at the whole picture, to say that the other animals have sensation but not what we mean by "thought". What we mean by "thought" involves making distinctions between past and present, between possible plans of action and between truth and falsehood, to mention no others. Everything seems to show that the other animals react to their environment in a sort of *automatic* way. They have built-in systems of instincts which are amazingly complex, but they cannot organise themselves and their environment in our sort of way. Something of immense importance is obviously missing, and it makes a difference to everything. Human awareness takes over the whole complex in which (on the basis of which) it arises and transforms it for its own purposes. It seems reasonable to say that the other animals do not even distinguish themselves from their environment in any proper sense of the words. In fact the only sense which we *can* give to the words is one which involves our human self-awareness and this is bound up with the whole human condition.

But does it mean anything to talk about "mere sensation"? If our human awareness takes it over, how can we pin it down in a pure state? It seems to me that we sometimes can. Take the case of "hearing the clock strike only after it has struck". In these circumstances our *attention* has been concentrated on other things. When we cease to concentrate we become *aware* of the sound and at the same time we want to say that it has been going on when we were *not* aware of it. How is so paradoxical a state of affairs to be explained? We might suggest that we had the sounds "in our minds" without adverting to them just as we are aware of our "selves" without adverting to them; but this does not seem true. We are aware of our "selves" as well as other things even without adverting to them; we are not aware of the clock striking at all until we attend to it. We can try to describe what happens to us only by saying that the sound comes to us from the past. We seem to look *back* to a sound previously heard. My proposal is that we have previously had the pure sensation of sound and that our awareness when it is turned on to it finds it as something already present, because not as something which is only here and now presenting itself. It is not what we mean by "sound" until we are aware of it. But something else, the *sensation* of which we are aware when we hear a sound, can be present before we are aware of it. It is possible, too, that in the twilight between sleeping and waking, that curiously impersonal state which some people at least would claim to have experienced, there is similar evidence.

Thus to say that the other animals live a life of pure sensation will be to say not that they have our awareness in some less developed form but that they do not have it at all. Their sensations are *signals* to which they respond in appropriate ways. When our awareness is brought to bear on sensations they function as *signs*; they reveal to us the behaviour of bodies. If such a distinction seems unacceptably sharp, it is perhaps because we are still haunted by the idea that all development is a gradual affair and that there can be no clean breaks. On the material level this principle may be sound enough; the human brain is historically continuous, no doubt, with non-human ones. But it does not follow that when a non-human brain has reached the appropriate stage of its development it cannot become the instrument of a higher power which comes to be on the basis of it, a power which requires it as a basis, and is thus dependent upon it in many ways, but which is a completely *new* power and produces a new situation. It is strange that people so often adopt extreme positions on the present topic. On the one hand, it is argued that cats and dogs, for instance, conduct reasoning processes and experience feelings of remorse. On the other hand, it is argued that the life of pure sensation is not special to the other animals but is really all that we ourselves enjoy, what we call our thoughts being only our talking to ourselves and our dispositions to act in this or that observable way : there are no private "mental acts". In the attempt to find a common formula for ourselves and the other animals theories on these lines are propounded which are entirely opposed to commonsense. What is still more to the point, they are either erected on a basis of no solid evidence or deny that evidence which we have actually before us.

It is not easy to be dispassionate on a topic which raises the ultimate question about our experience. If we are only jumped-up apes, then high-minded talk about morality or religion is inappropriate. Naturally people who take this view are irritated when they hear such talk. It also often alarms them because they fear that it is a danger to the well-being of the race or even to its survival. Why, on their showing, the individual should have to worry himself about other people's survival is not at all clear. In any case, on their showing, there seems nothing particularly interesting to survive for. People who believe that death is not the end for us, that we have a supernatural destiny, should react with equal vigour to the suggestion that the greatest of human achievements in art and in thought and in the conduct of life as a whole have been based on a mere illusion. I say that they *should* so react, because it is a very curious thing that so many people who hold this belief (or at any rate profess to hold it) seem to take little interest in the matter. And so many people seem content to remain in a state of half-belief about it—it is their apparent contentment which I find curious, not their hesitancy, for that is understandable enough in the present situation.

That prompts another general reflection. With so many conflicting opinions around and in an atmosphere of thought which seems predominantly irreligious, the chance of an individual's seeing his way clearly to a religious solution may appear very slim indeed. But that is not a properly balanced assessment of the position. If anyone is prepared to think for himself at all (and the most serious difficulty perhaps is that so few people are), it should become obvious that we cannot take the thought of our own time as necessarily sounder than the thought of other times. We know more facts than our ancestors did. But are these the facts which really matter? We can most of us employ techniques which were unknown to our grandfathers. But do they really make us any wiser? Furthermore it is just not true to say, even about our own time, that the religious solution is one of many competing solutions and that it has, on the face of it, no special claims upon our notice. The fact is that the other conflicting views are not offering *solutions* at all. This is becoming so widely recognised that it hardly needs arguing, but I shall return to it later. And although there are many conflicting opinions among religious people, belief in God is (when you consider the world as a whole) a phenomenon which bulks very large indeed, a solid block (although apparently less large than it was) against a welter of very diverse philosophical opinions. If we had only those diverse opinions to choose from we might well say that we could hardly be expected to cope. People who believe in God, however, do hold, by and large, some all-important conclusions in common. It is not at all unreasonable to ask whether they may not prove to be right. The chance that one might come to agree with them is not, after all, so very slim.

To return to the main line of this discussion, our experience is differentiated from that of other animals not solely by our *awareness* but also by our capacity for moral choice. What may be called the "commonsense" acount of free will is that when we are faced by alternative courses of action we are free to choose between them in the sense that our decision is not the inevitable result of our characters as so far formed and the pressure of circumstances upon us. We can resist this pressure and we can act out of character both for better and for worse, although this does not happen all that often. And we can realise what in the circumstances we *ought* to do and yet fail to do it by our own fault—we simply do not make the grade. According to another opinion, we are "free" only in the sense that the decision is made by ourselves and not forced upon us against our wills. It is *our* character and *our* present wants which decide what in fact we do. And these things being what they are, there is no question of our being able to do anything other than what we do in fact. The notion of moral failure, of personal responsibility, in what is still certainly the normal sense, is eliminated on this second account.

There is no argument in favour of the normal sense except that the facts of the matter are evident to us in our own experience, and notably in the fact that we are aware of ourselves on occasion as *failing* by our own choice here and now to make the grade. And, that being so, there is no place for further argument. To satisfy oneself about something one has to be *aware* of it, and if one *is* it is absurd to remain dissatisfied. Let us take a simple case. Suppose you have to get up in time to perform some important duty. When you wake you feel disinclined to get up. If you keep the need to do so before your mind, you may succeed in getting up. If you put it as far as possible out of your mind and allow the comforts of bed to exercise their attractions, then you will certainly stay there. There are two competing objects of desire. So long as they can be described as competing neither wins the day. Bed attracts in one way, the importance of the job in another. Up to a point we want to do our duty, but at the same time we want to stay in bed. If we really face the need to get up and accept it, then we shall be *really* wanting to do it and we *shall* do it, although we should have "preferred" to stay in bed—that is to say, we still find it disagreeable to get up and wish that it were unnecessary, but we realise that it is the better thing, the thing *called for,* in the circumstances. Thus we decide which is to be the stronger desire or the thing which we *really* want by giving our attention to it. The desire which wins must be the stronger one, but we can decide which it is to be. It is true that we must desire to do what we choose to do, but one of the things which we can desire to do is our duty, that is, what we recognise as the *good* thing for this occasion, the thing which will help to fulfil us.

Failing to follow the good, to do the right thing, is indeed a peculiar business. It is irrational, and we are naturally tempted to attribute it to causes outside ourselves ("something came over me"). This is no doubt very often the case when criminal actions are performed. But if we attend to our experience (and that is a necessary condition for understanding anything of this chapter) we can recognise quite plainly that there *are* occasions when we go through a process which can be "pointed to" rather than described by saying that we "throw in our hand" (with at least a part of our personality —there may well be another part which remains unwilling); there is an element of deliberation; we could have done better if we had kept our attention on what we could see to be in fact the right thing, if we had taken the trouble—and we *could* have taken the trouble. This *fact* of "closing down" on something is not to be explained away on grounds of heredity, social pressures or psychological quirks. This is another topic which is endlessly discussed but can never be settled by argument alone. Something has to be *seen.*

This brings us back to the topic of truth. Our claims to know the *truth* about anything are also said to be the result of social pressures. As someone once put it, there are really no hard facts, but all are more or less soft. We are back again at the question of *certainty.* The attack upon it from this new angle, instead of rejecting it because it cannot be proved by logical argument, takes the line of accepting it but interpreting it in a new way. According to this, we are perfectly entitled to dig ourselves in and to say that some statements cannot be doubted, but this is because in our particular historical circumstances, our language being what it is, it would be simply meaningless to cast doubt on their truth. A time might come, however, when it *would* mean something to do so. There are no timeless truths. I discuss this view in some detail in a later chapter, and here I am concerned only to point out that this way of dealing with the question of truth is just as repugnant to commonsense and just as disastrous as the account of "free will" which I have criticised. In each case our experience is interpreted in a way which robs it of its profundity.

When we say that we are aware of a world outside us, we are claiming that something is *true*. The suggestion that there could be circumstances in which it might prove not to be true would surely be rejected out of hand, we might suppose, by everyone. But a certain kind of philosopher will tell us that we are operating all the time with a bogus notion of truth. Should the existence of such philosophers make us wonder whether we understand what "true" ought to mean or whether perhaps we ought to give up using the word? It is plain to me, at any rate, that it stands for something which we cannot give up without stultifying ourselves. We do know that it means something to say "It is absolutely *true* that a war broke out in 1939"; it means that the evidence for it is entirely convincing, that nothing could ever occur which would falsify the statement. And it will *always* be true that the war broke out. It means something to say that too, although we may not realise at present just what it is. We could, of course, avoid the *word* "true" by always talking about "being certain" instead. But we cannot legitimately avoid the notion which we are in either case employing. It is the notion of being in touch with a state of affairs which really *is* what it declares itself to be. The age-old claim that you cannot avoid maintaining something as a fact whatever you say—even if it is that there *are* no facts—remains absolutely valid. To say that nothing is true is self-contradictory, that is, if we use "true" in the only way which makes sense.

But all this does show that there are questions about certainty to be faced. We ought not to say, if we want to be exact, that we *are certain* of anything if any possibility remains that we could be proved wrong. We can say that we *feel certain* about it if there is nothing before our minds which gives ground for doubting and all the evidence points in one direction. And this is the case about most of our conclusions. We *are* not certain, at least in the ordinary way, that the cook has not poisoned the food; we can only *feel* certain. Couldn't one *be* certain if the cook were one's wife? The question makes us realise that certainty in such cases depends on the extent of one's experience. A young boy may be uncertain that a war began in 1939; he has heard too little about it; to doubt it does not contradict what he does know to be true. (When he is older he could only doubt it by supposing that everyone is in league to make him believe a falsehood and—unless he can conclude that the world is a vast madhouse—he will in fact be certain of it.) But in any case he will be certain that there are other beings in the world besides himself. Some things are directly "before his mind".

There are two very common objections to this, of which I must make a first brief mention (they will be discussed at greater length later). One is that we can be in fact absolutely convinced of something and then find that it was untrue. How about the people who were convinced that the earth is flat? The answer, I should say, is that they were only taking it for granted; the possibility that it might be round had not been *excluded* by them because it had never occurred to them. If they did profess to exclude it, I should say that they did not understand the *import* of the question. The second objection is that it is always *logically* possible that one might be mistaken. This is really a variant of the demand for logical proof. But it takes the special form of saying that there is no contradiction in the notion that the cat might be not on the mat where I claim it to be, but somewhere else. The answer to this is that it is entirely irrelevant. It is a question not of notions but of facts. What I actually experience is *the truth*. I can be wrong about it only when I misinterpret it. Human experience, simply as such, is always *certain*.

Finally I want to make clear that I have not been proposing in this chapter a "dualism" of matter and spirit which denies any kinship between them. My concern here is not with some general notion of "spirit" but with human *awareness* as something which cannot be reduced to anything else. When I say that it differs from what preceded it in the evolutionary process not just in degree but in kind, I am not bound to suppose that the change-over was a startling one for the subject of it. There is no reason why it could not have been, so far as I can see. But it seems more consonant with the nature of things as we know it to suppose that it began in an embryonic form. I am, however, committed to saying that it *began*. There was a time when it had not come upon the scene and a time when it had. This causes difficulty for people who think that everything in our experience is a *process*, for it implies a mental event which occurs at a time but does not itself *take* time. I can only say that for me a mental event (a *seeing* of something) presents itself as having that character. Human awareness may have been preceded by a kind of "thinking" (there may have been makers of tools, for instance, who were not, in my sense of the word, *men*), and if it is claimed that (say) dogs and apes "think" in some such sense it does not affect my main contention. I have been using "consciousness" and "awareness" interchangeably, but if anyone wants to distinguish between them, reserving "awareness" for ourselves perhaps and speaking of the "consciousness" of other animals, I have no particular objection. All that matters at the moment is the claim that human awareness has certain characteristics : this is the necessary basis for the claim to an awareness of God.

"Belief" is a troublesome word, for it may mean something less than knowledge ("only a belief") or it may refer to knowledge in the strong sense, a definite awareness of something or somebody together with the implication that the object of this awareness is to be in some way *relied upon*. Religious belief is often supposed to deserve only the first of these meanings on the grounds that there are in fact no "supernatural" objects of which anyone could be aware and that religious people (except for a few cranks) do not even claim such awareness but just "bank on" the truth of some religious system or take it for granted without thinking about it at all because they happen to have been brought up that way. I shall propose that belief in God *can* be knowledge of him in the strong sense, although one may well receive the impression that this is seldom the case.

I have said that human experience, basically, is in itself an affair of certainty. In so far as we are really "in touch" with something, it is there. We do not merely take it for granted; we *know* it. How could this be the case when we are talking about "supernatural" objects? I shall prepare for an answer to this by considering first how "suspicion" can give place to "absence of doubt". When we have a "suspicion" about something, we are doubtful about how our experience is to be interpreted. For instance, I may hear a buzzing and I may not be sure whether it might not be something "in my head" instead of the effect upon me of something in the outer world. If the buzzing persists and I examine the situation closely I may be able to satisfy myself one way or the other. Or perhaps I may become only "pretty sure" that it is caused by the heating system. If other people assure me that this is in fact the case I may come to have no doubt about it at all. Even so I still have no absolute proof. For to have absolute proof that another body is affecting my own I need to be unambiguously aware of it *as* doing so.

It seems to me that very many people believe in God in the sort of way in which I imagined myself believing in the cause of the buzzing. Everything, they may think, points that way. It makes sense of their experience as a whole, and there seem to be others (the first Christians, for instance) for whom it was a fact of sheer experience, a certainty. It seems the right conclusion to reach. They commit themselves to this belief. This should not be taken to mean that they pretend to a certainty which in fact they do not possess or that they make the impossible attempt to force one upon themselves (although of course such things do happen). It means that they adopt certain practices. In particular, they pray—it makes perfectly good sense to ask whether somebody is there and to give him the chance to declare himself. And if they keep up this practice they may become clearer — indeed certain — on the matter.

Such people may tell you that the God whom they have come to acknowledge proves to have been present all along, although they had not realised that it was so. (That is, they are referring to something in their experience, not to a conclusion that some power *must* be always acting upon us to keep us in being.) If they are right, then it is possible for a man to have had some awareness of God not only when there was a "suspicion" of him but even before that arose. They are saying that they have been aware of something for as long as they can remember which they did not originally connect with God at all but which they now recognise as his activity in them. They may describe this "something" in different ways. The suggestion is that an awareness of God is congenital to the human mind, although it will not be recognised at first for what it is. It may present itself in more than one form.

The form in which it can be most easily recognised, for most people, is the moral form : that is, the fundamental characteristics of our moral experience; and I shall therefore discuss it at some length. But first I must prepare the way for it. In the last chapter I maintained that the experience of moral freedom cannot be explained away as the result of historical accidents. Some people will say that they have no such experience or that they have only a "feeling" of freedom which cannot be relied upon as good evidence. When questions of this kind arise a stock move (and a sound one) from the other side is to adduce a parallel from the appreciation of the arts. Anyone who doubts whether there is anything objective in music and painting to account for the value attached to these things by others would be well advised, so some of us would say, to suspect that there is something lacking in himself rather than to suppose that the others are playing up or somehow producing from their own resources the cause of their interest and enjoyment. Disbelieving in moral freedom (in the sense of an ability to go *against* one's existing character one way or the other) is still a relatively rare phenomenon (and is commonly bound up with a general disbelief in the validity of human experience). Accepting it will not of itself settle the ultimate questions. But it seems reasonable to suppose that it may rouse a first suspicion that our moral experience has some profound significance.

To be morally responsible means that we *ought* to do certain things and avoid others. The suggestion that "ought" is due to sociological causes is sound enough up to a point. It is no doubt true that people do feel some obligations which are just the automatic result of their training and their antecedents. When they discover that this is so, they should have no great difficulty in casting off these burdens, unless they should find good reasons for them (in which case they will cease to be just burdens). But there are some obligations which seem to be bound up with the nature of things. Human beings are thought to have "rights". They ought not to be treated just as providing us with opportunities for gratifying our whims. But why not? It may be said that this can be explained as necessary for the survival of the race. But why *ought* the individual to bother himself about the survival of the race? Or is it suggested that he cannot help doing so? That is plainly untrue. The other animals have instincts over which they have no control. So have we, but the instinct to keep the race in being is not one of them. There are certainly people around who manage to take no interest in it. It is indeed "natural" to love our fellow men. But it is only too clear that we are not forced to do so. Trying to reduce "ought" to "must" will not do.

There are times, indeed, when we use "ought" to mean a kind of "must". "I ought to go if I am to catch my train" means that it is necessary for me to go if I am to catch it. There is no necessity of *this* kind about "ought" in the moral sense. When you are faced with an obligation, you are physically free to accept or reject it. There is a demand made upon you—an insistent invitation—but it is addressed to your freedom. It seems a very curious thing that this state of affairs should be regarded simply as a sort of brute fact or a dead end for thought. But that seems to be a point of view largely if not wholly confined to academic circles. The reply that most people do not reflect on the matter at all and might accept this academic view if they did seems to me unconvincing. Very many people, I should say, including people who have no use for religion, do attach a peculiar importance to moral decisions and a peculiar value to moral uprightness which they do not indeed theorise about but which they recognise in however vague a way as opening up mysterious issues.

Recognising that other people have "rights" is the obvious starting-point for an enquiry into "ought". It seems that there is something about them which makes a claim on us. It may not be at all clear what this is. Can we find anything in *ourselves* which sheds any light? Is there some claim on us as individuals, something which we are all called upon to do *about* ourselves, which may provide a clue? What does it mean to say that we find *value* in ourselves, something which we have to acknowledge, some claim on our attention? (When I say we "have to", I do not mean that we cannot dismiss this claim or that it comes into operation as an instinct does.) We may recognise that we have certain capacities and that we have to use them if we are to achieve our ambitions. But that does not constitute a *moral* demand. If, however, we do nothing to develop these capacities, do we merely regret that our ambitions are unattainable, giving them up as requiring too much effort? It is a state of mind which is certainly possible. But is it one in which we *ought* to remain? This is the point, I think, at which "ought" reappears in a form which it is hardest to escape from and which can reveal its ultimate significance. We are not entitled simply to throw away the powers which we recognise as our own. If this ultimate moral claim is rejected anyone who wants to talk about God's presence in man will have to try another tack at least for the time being.

But there is more to be said about it by way of explaining how it can be the sign of God's presence. From a Christian's point of view God would be expected to communicate somehow with his intelligent creatures, and not only with those to whom the Christian revelation is addressed. If he summons all men to him at all times, as Christians believe, does he do this in the first instance simply by presenting them with the spectacle of the material universe from which they are expected to "read off" his existence? (There is hardly anyone left nowadays who supposes that it can be done by a process of sheer logic, based on the facts of the finite world alone : you cannot *argue* the Infinite into your experience.) I am not denying that God can be thus "read off". But I suggest that such a process needs to be accompanied, and indeed, I think, preceded, by an awareness of God as present to our own spiritual being. (I shall be going into that more fully later.) A Christian will say, moreover, that God is not just the creator of the world but man's *end,* his fulfilment. It is to be expected, then, that when man appears on the scene it will be the capacity to grasp that he has such an end which, in the last analysis, makes him what he is. He will know himself as attracted to *the good*. This is his reaction to an awareness of what is in fact God's action upon him, his summons to fulfilment, although it is not yet articulated in these terms (or not articulated at all).

An awareness of God's action must be an awareness of *God himself as acting*. Just as we cannot be aware of the external world unless it enters our experience (in our awareness of our own bodies, where it is present in its activity), so, if we are aware of God, he must enter our experience in his activity, whether we find him in the world outside or in ourselves. We are directly aware of ourselves in our activities. And we are aware of ourselves as in tension towards some undefined project. In other words, we are aware of something which pulls us towards it. We are aware of it very dimly —and the dimness leaves us dissatisfied, whether in the sense that at first we only *suspect* that there is something there (could it be our "imagination"?) or in the sense that we are aware of impediments to a kind of real beholding which has already begun and want them removed. This state of affairs makes sense on the hypothesis that God calls men to the knowledge and love of him. Does it make sense on any other hypothesis?

I cannot see that it does. If "ought" is to be accepted as a reality at all and not reduced to something else, then this fundamental instance of it, on which all others seem to depend, must be a recognition that my life has a purpose—one which I have not given to it myself. For to say that life has a purpose cannot mean just that the universe pursues its course according to certain predictable regular rhythms, that it has produced ourselves and that we can now do all sorts of things with it. If we held the view that it is capable of producing a race of super-men there might be more excuse for such language, but even if we pin our hopes on some power not ourselves, working for survival and development, there seems to be no reason why we should feel obliged to co-operate with it. To say that it is just a "natural urge" is to return either to accepting obligation as just a brute fact which for some mysterious reason is not always acknowledged or to explaining it away as a sort of by-product of genetic and environmental factors. To acknowledge obligation, to recognise oneself as morally bound, summoned as a person, either to a life-force or to a "moral order", a mysterious impersonal sphere which issues arbitrary commands, is surely not a sensible thing to do. It makes better sense to reject this summons as an illusion and to write off our situation as "absurd". If it is something which belongs to human nature as such and has an *absolute* quality, we must interpret it in terms of an absolute person.

At this point I should make clear that I am not putting forward the argument from conscience which has been commonly employed by religious apologists. That argument presupposes the existence of moral laws and infers from them the existence of a legislator. I am not concerned for my present purposes with particular moral laws but with the fact that there is a fundamental moral situation on which they are all based : an awareness of God as man's end from which our moral freedom derives (we have to grow into love for him, and he cannot force love upon us). Nor am I building an *argument* on the facts of the moral consciousness, but pointing to the presence of God as what we are really apprehending even when we might describe ourselves simply as somehow bound to uphold certain principles (those of justice and compassion, for instance). On this showing so many "agnostics" are truly "in touch" with God. In practice, "conscience" can mean more than one thing. But a moment's thought shows that it is not some faculty distinct from the mind. It is just my experience recognising itself as on the move to a goal, and my judgement, that being so, on what the present circumstances demand of me. (But it is not just *my* goal : we are all in it together, and this circumstance always makes its demand.) Conscience, then, is not "just a feeling". Supposing that it is naturally makes people suspicious about moral evidence—so does the wide variety of moral systems and stances. I am trying to indicate something of which we can be as certain as we are of ourselves, because it can be *seen* to be a part of ourselves, something without which we should not be men at all.

It may be useful to return to the language of *value* about it. There is a way of seeing things as valuable when we are not proposing to use them for our private purposes but just recognising that they "have something". Some things *ought* to be preserved, for instance, because they are so beautiful. They make a claim on us to recognise them for what they are. The *absolute* quality, to which I have already referred, seems to shine through them. We can go on, I think, to recognise, if we give our attention to this, that this quality does not belong to them in their own right. It comes from "beyond". If this is so, then what else can we say than that they are manifestations, created and finite, of an infinite source of reality? To this I shall return. I mention it here because it may help to explain the attitude which we do in fact so often adopt to things and more particularly to persons when they make the moral demand on us which in its basic form arises in our own self-consciousness.

It is surely the case that the ultimate question is regularly put in the form : has life a meaning? And I have suggested that this will reduce in the end to the question : can I find a meaning in my own experience? If there is an answer to this, I have concluded, it must lie in the discovery of God. And this discovery, I have said, can take more than one form. That is to say, the presence of God may be explicitly recognised under more than one aspect. So far I have considered the awareness of God as found in the basic moral reaction which it sets up in us. Now I want to make another approach by returning to the topic of truth which was adumbrated in the first chapter.

It is possible to feel completely bewildered by the questions which we are here considering. There may seem to be so much persuasive argument on both sides. And it may also seem supremely important to get at the *truth* if one can. This could be because it is so difficult to get on with anything in particular until you know where you stand in a general way. But there is more to it than that. The truth seems to matter, as it were, for its own sake (and nothing can so matter, it may be added, unless it is true—value is truth, to adapt Keats, and truth value). This, I shall submit, is another way in which God's presence in the world is manifested.

Take the case of someone who has come to feel that the religion in which he has been brought up may well be without support in reason. His experience seems to tell him nothing. He has concluded, rightly or wrongly, that anything in the nature of religious experience which he may have thought himself to possess was in fact mere sentimentalism. We may suppose that his religious education has been an unintelligent one. Eventually he feels bound to give up the whole business of religion. There are too many reasons against it. In his case it is not that he wants to give it up at the start or wants not to give it up. He just feels *bound* to accept what comes to appear the truth to him. He is not *certain* that religion is a hoax, but he no longer feels any real doubt that it is and he gives it up accordingly. He is following his conscience. He is accepting the good as he sees it. He knows that there is something called truth which demands his acceptance. (In this case it requires him to acknowledge the breakdown of his childhood beliefs.) He submits to it—and this is, I hold, an act of worship. He has not really given up religion, although this is what he is purporting to do. He is starting to build up a religious life—from the ground floor. Even though he is mistaken in thinking that truth is opposed to any form of religion, he is *worshipping* in doing what he supposes it to require of him.

This illustrates what should be meant by saying that God judges men according to their consciences. If they are really *aiming* at the truth, they are in the right way. They can lose God only by turning from the truth (whether or not they have explicitly recognised the Infinite in it) and this can take the form of being dishonest with themselves, as the man in our story was tempted to be. Incidentally it should now seem decidedly odd that Christians sometimes reject this view about God's actual *presence* in the conscience. For how else are some men to *choose* him (as they must if they are to attain to him in the end) unless they can find him there? Even the most ignorant and the most muddled must have their opportunity, sometime and somehow. For some this opportunity does not arise, perhaps, until the moment of death brings them face to face with it, but we can hardly accept this as the norm.

Moral awareness, like all awareness, is awareness of the truth. Accepting the "ought" is accepting the truth, and this is the fundamental moral action. It is the aspect of *the good* which, so to say, normally "strikes" people first, so I have supposed. But in fact it depends upon *the truth*.

In the first chapter I tried to show that the notion of truth cannot be legitimately evaded (in other words, it *can* be, but it *ought* not to be) and that it has an "ordinary" meaning, although a mysterious one, which can be denied only verbally, not in actual fact. "It is true that . . ." does mean something. It is time to enquire what it is. It does not mean just that things will let us down if we do not acknowledge their "truth", if we treat what we find to be "the case" as if it were not the case. Finding what is the case about the way to make the kettle boil does not mean just that it will be awkward for you unless you treat it that way. It means that it is part of the way in which things are constituted that the kettle will respond suitably only in certain conditions. It is something to do, we have to say, with *reality*, and that is not a "metaphysical" notion which we can get rid of with a little ingenuity. It makes all the difference whether something is really there in the world outside or whether it is only an "idea" in our minds. To say

23

that something *is* does not, indeed, describe it in any way, but it says something quite definite about it. Things are not true just because they *work*; they could not work unless they were really (truly) there.

So when we say that something *is* there, we say that it belongs to reality. It is part of the furniture of the universe. If in some sense it will always be true that it was there, this may serve as a "pointer" to an eternal mind in which our past, present and future are somehow "contained". It is at least not clear that we can make sense of it otherwise. But in any case when we say that something *is* there now we are saying that it is established in reality and, I believe, we are implying, although we may not be explicitly aware of it, that it derives from the source of reality. This may be brought out, perhaps, in the following way. When we say that something *is*, we make a statement not just about a part of it but about the whole of it. And such a statement has to be made about anything at all which we could come across. Since "is" applies to everything and to every part of everything, it cannot be a *quality* which everything has, for in that case it would be a description of just one *part* which is common to everything. Put it like this : if "is" refers to something which things have in common, then, since it refers in fact to *everything* about them, there would be nothing left to make them *different* from one another. The only conclusion which seems left is that "is" refers to a relationship in which they all stand to a "beyond". And if this is not the relationship in which created things stand to their Creator I do not know what it can be.

That is a very abstract sort of analysis, and it may therefore fail to make much impact or sound like a piece of legerdemain which the experts might easily unmask. In fact I am not aware that anyone has done so. You can try to get round it, so far as I can see, only by saying that we use "is" as a convenient way of indicating things which we claim to know, not meaning to suggest that it *belongs* to them in any way—so that they have nothing in common among themselves except for the fact that we happen to come across them, and this has no effect upon *them*. In other words, a relationship emerges once more, but it is one in which *we* stand to the objects of our knowledge, and it would follow that the problem which *they* seemed to set us does not in fact arise. This seems to me a desperate expedient. To say that something *is* there certainly means that I am aware of it. But it is, I suggest, plain that it does not refer simply to *my* knowledge but also, somehow, to *it* in itself.

To say that my knowledge has no effect upon it is certainly right. But must we not say, therefore, that it leaves it as it *is*?

Still, it is all very abstract. My proposal can be put in a way which may prove more effective as a "pointer" (the previous analysis is also only a "pointer", however plausible, because it is possible to get round it, however implausibly). When we experience something and are certain of it, we make an *absolute* claim. I have already referred to an "absolute" quality which some people or things seem to have—or rather which seems to "shine through them", and I have suggested that this indicates their *derivation* from—and so their dependence upon—an absolute source. The present suggestion is that the absoluteness of knowledge is to be interpreted along the same lines. We are in touch with God not only in our moral aspirations and in our intimations of absolute perfection but also in the basic awareness on which these depend. When we are certain of anything and say that it is absolutely true, we are saying, on this view, that it is grounded on the absolute and that we in knowing it are grounded on the absolute. This becomes clear, if it does, only by taking a good look at it (that goes, I must again insist, for all attempts to bring to explicit consciousness the awareness of God which I hold to be implicitly operative in all specifically human activities). As an attempt to bring out this character of our basic awareness I shall say that when we are certain of something, when we come across what is here and now infallibly and indefeasibly a reality, we are aware of *the other* as an immovably solid foundation. And *this* "otherness" is not simply that of bodies interfering with our own. It is a solidity for which neither these bodies nor ourselves account. We are not infallible nor are they indefeasible in virtue of resources originating from ourselves and themselves.

It is difficult to talk about this without falling into esoteric language. The awareness of which I am trying to speak cannot be properly described because you can properly describe a thing only in terms of something which is akin to it—or of some quality already known—and our awareness of God is unique. Although simple in itself, it may be very difficult to recognise. That calls for *attention*. What has to be recognised is God's action upon us, *giving* us our awareness. In knowing ourselves and finite objects we are (however dimly and inarticulately) aware of him also, and thus when we register them and say that they *are* we relate them to him. As I see it, this awareness of him is *rooted* in his action upon ourselves, not in the finite objects on which he is also acting. We do find him in them but only when we have learned to recognise his activity in our own powers of knowing. It is not all-important, however, to insist on this last precision if it seems to cause difficulty. What matters is the recognition, however exactly it is thought to come about, that both ourselves and everything else are totally *dependent*, deriving from the source of reality. There is often talk about a *"feeling* of dependence", especially among Protestant theologians. I want to speak of an *apprehension* of God in his empowering of ourselves and of all things.

If the suspicion that this is the case arises, it may be strengthened by recalling what has been said already about knowledge, that when we know anything it in some sense makes us what we are for the time being, while remaining unchanged itself, that there is a union of the knowing subject with the object known such that there is nothing separating them and yet they remain sheerly distinct, that we have to submit ourselves to what we come to know and allow it (as it were) to work its will on us. It must be borne in mind that the notion of truth comes first (that of a mistake or that of a mere probability being intelligible only in terms of it). When to this is added that truth in its ordinary meaning, which is the only acceptable one, includes the fact that it is available for all minds, that it is in principle public property, then it may appear that this mysterious language about knowledge, which gives offence to many modern philosophers, is not only forced upon us by our experience but is also positively significant. If a definitive union with God is postulated as the term towards which the growth of our knowledge is directed, it may become clear in time that an awareness of God as found in his creatures is the principle which presides over our whole experience.

It may also become clear that we cannot keep knowledge and love in watertight compartments. Seeing something as good or beautiful, admitting it without restriction into one's experience, must be called loving it. Turning away from it because attending to it is too much trouble is refusing one's love. Awareness comes first, but without love it will not grow. And since it is its business to grow, without love it cannot be itself. Awareness, in other words, is of its nature free. That is, in principle we can do what we like with it, although in the first instance it is a gift which we find present. We cannot really conceive of ourselves as *unfree* as regards the use of it. And man is a natural ecstatic. It is his business to be absorbed in *the other,* and this is also his own self-development. All this can make sense if the end is union with God.

If there is a suspicion of this, *ought* it not to be followed up? To reject the suspicion is not to reject God absolutely because there is only a suspicion of him. But that does make a certain claim on us. How is it to be followed up? The only answer in the long run, it would appear, is that it must be *attended to.* We are back again to the agnostic's (or rather the doubter's) prayer. It is unlikely to produce a sudden and complete illumination, although this does sometimes occur. When it produces conviction (perhaps only after a long time) it often seems to have done so imperceptibly—a man finds that he has already started believing.

I have offered an outline sketch of how, as I see it, God first makes contact with the human mind or soul. Obviously it is a topic which could be discussed at indefinite length. But I must soon pass on to topics which are closely bound up with it. One has been looming over the whole of this chapter. That is the claim that there are sufficient reasons for *disallowing* the question about God. At any rate, it will be said, if the source of reality were the God in whom Christians believe, the world would not be in its present appalling condition. I shall discuss that in the next chapter. And another question arises to which the first part of that chapter will be devoted : what right have I to identify this source of reality with the God in whom Christians believe? Do I, in other words, assign to it the attributes of the Christian God and, if so, on what grounds? So far what I mean by God has been indicated by my analysis of the fundamental characters of our experience (and if that analysis seems to have no upshot I could only attempt it again in different language and perhaps from a different starting-point). Such an analysis, it must be insisted, is in any case only a beginning. It may come to mean more when we reach the end of the story.

But there is something to be added here about this whole approach to the evidence, for it is one which is less familiar in this country than abroad (and perhaps specially unfamiliar to most English Catholics). It concerns my attitude to the efficacy of logical argument in this matter. I have remarked that there is scarcely any thinker nowadays who supposes that God could emerge as the conclusion of some cast-iron logical process based on simple acknowledged facts about the world around us. Nevertheless there are plenty of people who would not *call themselves* "thinkers" and who suppose that logical arguments are at least an essential part of the business, although perhaps not the whole of it. Even if they accept my contention that to be sure of anything we must be ourselves in touch with it (or with others on whose information we can wholly rely), they may still feel that the "traditional" arguments, by which is meant usually the "Five Ways" of Saint Thomas Aquinas, ought to be discussed. These all appeal to causality in one way or another. They draw our attention to certain features of the world around us with a view to making clear that it is not self-explanatory. That is what I have been doing here, although my emphasis is on the knower in the first place rather than on the known. It is open to question how far, in the view of Saint Thomas himself, his arguments take us simply as logical processes. I must give my reasons for regarding such arguments as not formally cogent.

A supposedly cast-iron logical argument for God will reduce to this : there is a law of thought, a principle of causality, according to which when anything *happens* it is caused by something else—so the universe must have a Cause. Apart from the fact that this principle is not obvious to everybody ("the universe itself *just* happened—there is no need to ask questions about it"), putting it like this makes God an instance (even if the supreme instance) of a general rule. And it should be clear that God is not an *instance of* anything. The "principle of causality" can only be an unfortunate way of talking about God himself. The argument presupposes what it purports to prove. Unless the Infinite is somehow contained in the argument's starting-point it cannot emerge in the conclusion. This is true of all versions of the causal argument when it is supposed to be of the cast-iron type. And thus I conclude that in order to get "in touch" with the cause you have to *find* it *in* its actual operation (to repeat, we should not know that sensations are caused by a world outside unless they put us in touch with it *in* its action upon us).

Highly influential theologians, however, in recent centuries have taken it as a principle that our knowledge of God is, at least in its origins, always *indirect,* the conclusion of a logical process, and this attitude of mind has lasted up to our own times. This has had the deplorable consequence that the real evidence for God, our direct awareness of him, has been widely disregarded. It has also resulted in the mistaken belief that those who claim such a direct awareness are not orthodox Christians. The distinction between a *direct* and an *immediate* knowledge of God has not been grasped. There is no claim to the unclouded vision of God, which is impossible while we are in the present body. Our knowledge of him is very much clouded as a rule by our *immediate* knowledge, by the medium *in* which we apprehend him, ourselves and our world. The *directness* of all awareness of God is the theme which runs through this book. At present I am discussing it only in its initial form.

From a Christian's point of view it should be easy to see that the God whom he worships makes an anonymous appearance in the moral lives of non-Christians. But non-Christians might see little or no connection between their experience and the God of Christians, even if they were to grant that there is something *absolute* involved in it. The God of Christians, they might say, has characteristics which raise special problems : he is not only a creator, but also free to create or not to create; he is both just and merciful at the same time, to take only these examples of the difficulties which beset the notion of a personal God; and when it comes to the content of "revelation", we are told that he is not one person but three, that he became a man . . . There is no need to go on. Those last difficulties must be postponed for discussion in later chapters. Here I shall try to indicate, and only, of course, in broadest outline, how the apprehension of the Absolute can be held to contain implicitly a belief in the Creator whose characteristics have been summed up in the one word "love".

I have already proposed that the invasion of our experience by the Absolute leads us to recognise our own complete dependence upon it as the source of reality. But this recognition does not always take place, notoriously, when the Absolute is acknowledged. And in thinking about it how is one supposed to make the move from "it" to "he"?

In the first place there is a possible confusion to be avoided. Sometimes it is supposed that a "personal" God must be a limited one. But this is to forget that words which are used of God are never strictly descriptions of him. Even the phrase "source of reality" will not be of itself informative about who God is. Unless there is an awareness of him, it will not be understood that he is "beyond" the world in a unique sense to which we can only point by using negative terms. "Infinite" is the regular one. For the believer it has a positive sense—or rather the Infinite is absolute positivity because it is the ground of all that is apprehended as such. But he cannot directly communicate this sense; he can only invite people to look for it. So instead of speaking about a "personal" God he may try to point to what he means by calling him "super-personal". ("Supra-personal" would amount to "impersonal".) This means not only that God has none of the limitations which attach to human personality but also that he has in an infinite, unlimited form all the values which we find in personality. It is the recognition of this which leads to the use of the personal pronoun (and it is the moral aspect of our awareness of God which leads us most directly, I have suggested, to this conclusion).

Why, then, is this so often not recognised by people who do acknowledge the Infinite in a positive sense? Christians can have no doubt that there are "monists" who have a genuine apprehension of the Absolute although they reject the implications which Christians find in it. They are not so common among thinkers in the West as they were in the early years of the century, but they are very numerous indeed in the East. It is baffling to the typical Western mind that people should seem to regard human beings and their environment as somehow *parts* of the Absolute or even as illusions, the Absolute being the only reality. If there is to be talk of the Absolute at all, it seems obvious that it cannot have *parts*—an assemblage of parts must be limited, for you can always add to it. It seems equally obvious that an "Absolute" which itself develops is also limited. And unless we give up the attempt to make sense of things, how can we fail to recognise our own personalities as distinct from one another and from everything else? If these are not realities, we cannot speak of reality at all. (But God is not *a* reality : he is the source of reality; in affirming ourselves, we affirm him also.) So when we hear people saying that "everything is all one really", we may find ourselves simply baffled.

But one can perhaps make a suggestion. There is a long tradition in the East which is opposed to "dualism", that is, to a view of things which leaves two realities, finite and infinite, opposed irreducibly to one another. The Christian view does oppose finite and infinite irreducibly in the sense that the notion of reality is irreducibly double—to be real or to exist means to derive from the source : the derived existence and the source are affirmed as irreducibly distinct. But it is also the Christian view that man is made in the *image* of God, and it is a regular theme of Christian thought that all God's creatures are created manifestations of him. They "resemble" him in a way which is (necessarily) unique. Whatever we find as valuable in the world must be found in him in its original, unlimited form. God's creatures are not merely dependent on him for their existence but also linked with him in this relationship of "likeness", which indeed makes them *what* they are. In the West there has been so much concentration on the transcendence of God that this relationship has been left in the shade, and thus the full richness of the doctrine of creation is often not properly appreciated—especially in the East, where it seems to be thought necessary to reject the reality of the finite as the only way to avoid compromising the Infinite. If Easterners are to be charged with a failure here, it is a magnificent one. Western secularisers must reckon with the massive Eastern witness to the Absolute and its conviction that nothing else matters.

The Christian doctrine of the creation, however, has to face the further difficulty that according to it God is free to create or not to create and it is said to make no difference to him whether he creates or not. Either way he is just what he unchangeably is. But does this make any sense? Here we are reminded to control our imaginations. If we picture God's creating as an event in time, then it must make a difference to him. If it is a timeless one, then there was no time for God when his act of creation had not yet occurred and the difficulty disappears. But it remains that, if God chose not to create (which is said to be a possibility for him), he *would* be different, for the act of creating is *his* act and without it he would not be what he is. It seems to me, then, that we must avoid making God's freedom mean "choosing": we must not think of God as faced by alternatives (or by an infinity of possible worlds), for his freedom is all-creative. We must say, I think, that there is no question of God's *not* creating, that for him to be super-generous is just for him to be *himself*. But he does not *need* to create—that is, he does not need his creatures to provide himself with something which he would not otherwise possess, and it is surely this on which Christian teaching insists when it insists on his freedom. He creates because, being God, he *gives*. This difficulty about God's "choosing" is commonly dodged by Christian thinkers, and that is, I believe, a reason why the doctrine of creation is unacceptable to many, in the East especially but also in the West. If I am right, we have to say that the world is not one of many possible worlds but just God's world.

When we are told that there are relationships between creatures and God but not between God and creatures, this must mean that God is not affected by his creatures. But that cannot mean that he takes no interest in them but rather that he takes an infinite interest in them, that his attitude is one of unlimited and unchanging beneficence. This conception is admittedly not without its own difficulties, and I shall return to it.

There is also the fact that an explicit awareness of God as creator does not appear in any big way outside the Judaeo-Christian tradition or those which derive from it. A Christian, however, finds no difficulty in holding that the powers of the human mind needed to be restored by the effects of Christ's coming, for they had become weakened. And here it may be suggested that the men of the ancient world were "in touch" with God through their moral experience in a way which was perhaps more effective than their official religious exercises—to go further into their state of mind would demand a whole history of ancient thought and especially its theories of cosmogony.

The topic of creation has led me to touch on some important themes which need to be more closely examined. In what follows it has to be borne in mind that I am describing a process of exploration, the gradual penetration of a datum which lies at the heart of our experience, the making explicit of what was implicit and inarticulate. It is a process which, as we have just had occasion to notice, can be held up or sidetracked by a variety of causes, and it requires the *attention* to which I have more than once referred, that is, an active and persistent openness of mind and a freedom from preconceived notions rather than mental acumen or any sort of technical competence. I have raised a number of questions about God's "attributes" by speaking of the "infinite form" in which all values are found in him, and before saying anything about particular "attributes" I must say something more about the way in which, as I see it, we reach that general conclusion. It seems to me that when an apprehension of the Absolute occurs there is, in the first place, the discovery of the Infinite Other but that this is accompanied (if our attention is unimpeded) by the discovery that the Other is nevertheless not *alien* to ourselves and to our environment. And what I now need to emphasise is that this discovery does not result from any process of argument but is bound up with the original apprehension itself. God's "attributes" are not *deduced* from a notion of infinity or self-existence. We cannot know *that* God is without knowing something of *who* he is and, since we cannot throw light on God's "nature" by any appeal to general principles, we have to concentrate, if we are to get any further, on that knowledge of *who* he is.

This consideration is so central for the whole discussion that I must pause upon it for a moment. The situation which we are envisaging is unique. We have to take it as we find it, and notions brought in from outside will be no help to us. For example, we cannot argue that all causes must in some sense "contain" their effects, for we have only to think of what we call "causes" in our everyday affairs to realise that they do nothing of the kind. We have to conclude, I think, that the notion of a cause which is solely responsible for the production of its effect and "contains" the virtue of it in fact derives from the apprehension of God. To repeat, we can only "point to" the apprehension of the Other. And until that apprehension has occurred to speak of "manifestations" or "reflections" will be useless. They are intelligible only in the light of it. So it is misleading to say that we can gain knowledge of God by starting with (say) the notion of finite goodness and then "removing its imperfections". It suggests that you can build up the Infinite out of the finite. That is what seems to be said by people who suppose that you can "prove God's existence" and then work out what his attributes must be, although how they (so to speak) function remains, they say, completely unknown to us.

And that makes necessary a further general consideration about the convergence of values at infinity. It seems to me that if we are entitled to talk about God's "attributes" at all, we must *glimpse* a simplicity which is also a fullness, a unity which is refracted in our knowledge of it into different aspects but which is itself unbroken. But it is plainly true that this always remains for us profoundly mysterious. We glimpse the convergence of values, but we do not (to speak strictly) *share* God's life at all. We are "in touch" with him, but our knowledge is brought up against darkness.

Now at last it is possible to face the objections to what I have been saying. First, isn't this alleged convergence of values in fact unthinkable, a contradiction? That must be to say that there is something in our experience which rules it out. If we *do* know something, we know that nothing can rule it out, and if anything purports to do so we rule *that* out—the "law" of contradiction is simply a general formula for such situations. There can be no proof that the claim to an awareness of the convergence of values can be ruled out in principle. (I am not suggesting that it is easily attainable, but it is not so hard to conclude that some people have attained it—the outstanding witness of the great mystics should be at least encouraging to those who have some faint inkling or "suspicion" of it.) But when we consider particular "attributes", surely we run into insuperable difficulties?

Let us, then, take the question of God's mercy and his justice. There is no difficulty about his mercy: it is his unchanging beneficence. His justice, in the language of the New Testament, is his fidelity to his promises—there is no difficulty about that. But it also means "giving us our deserts". Now it is a commonplace of Christian theology that God never abandons us but that we can abandon him (this, of course, leads to the difficulties discussed in the second part of the chapter). "Giving us our deserts", then, means that God, having given us our freedom, does not take it back. Love is always his meaning, even though it puts us at risk. Thus the claim is that all the values of personality which we find in him fuse into his generosity and that there is nothing to rule this out. But what about the values which we find in the world around us? What counts there as a value, as something which has its foundation in the Absolute? Everything, I suggest, in so far as it is not spoiled by sin. (Or is there, in the last analysis, anything else which can spoil things? Again I must refer to the subsequent discussion.) In a book of this kind I must be content with this summary reply, adding only that to speak of absolute beauty seemed inevitable to the first great teacher of the West and that this doctrine of Platonism has always been a part of Christian thought.

But there are certain special difficulties which are felt very keenly at the present time. The language traditionally used of God seems to make him static and lifeless. One may find this surprising, since he has been so regularly "pointed to" as "pure act", infinite energy. But the objection is that this pointer does not work. If God's activity is "pure", this can mean only that it has come to a stop, for all life is process and so if God is not a process he is nothing. I have said that a God who develops would be obviously a limited one, not *God* at all. But it is contended that development is itself a value. It seems to me that we have to make a distinction here. Development is a value in so far as it is the increment of life. In so far as it involves a *lack* of what is still to come, it carries with it limitation. All our life is process, but God is the *source* of life. That is what "pure act", which is the same as "pure life", is saying. For again we have to remember that such words are only "pointers" and that the apprehension which provokes them is a unique one, standing (so to speak) on its own feet. If to say that something exists does mean that it derives from the Source, we cannot even say properly "God exists". We *affirm* him as beyond existence.

The objection which we have been considering is often pressed in terms of God's changelessness and timelessness, which seem unthinkable, it is said, except as a standing still. How can one inject life into timelessness without importing *duration* into it? Again it seems to me that the *value* of duration is not succession but activity, and although it is obviously impossible to *imagine* an activity which does not involve succession it is not impossible to think it or rather to glimpse it. And this is not a reducing of successive activity to an eternal moment or point. It is glimpsing the timeless across time as a *fullness*. It is perhaps impossible not to use the imagination here, but so long as we realise that it is not at bottom the business of the imagination this can be a help rather than a hindrance. A picture of God as encompassing the changing world instead of shrinking to a point is a natural consequence of an apprehension of him as the unlimited. It must be repeated that this is not to make a claim to *share* God's timeless life. Even in the next world it would seem that it is always "beyond" us, for we can never exhaust the Infinite, and our "eternal life" must be an ever-deepening love.

All this goes to show that when we speak of God we have to use language which is, taken at its face value, contradictory, accompanied by images which conflict with one another. God "contains", we have to say, the values both of fulfilment and of freshness. He is both ever-old and ever-new. He is both necessary, in the sense that he cannot be other than he is, and free, in the sense that he is pure spontaneity. Our concepts break out beyond their original limitations and begin to merge with one another. Talk of a "higher synthesis" is often bogus, but not here. This, we find, is what we *mean* by "the Infinite".

The topics which I have been discussing have often been discussed in terms of "analogy". I have avoided this language because I did not want it supposed that I was advancing a "theory of analogy". What I have been concerned with is matter of fact, not theory. "Analogy" has sometimes been produced (with the air of a conjuror producing a rabbit out of a hat) as a happy mean between talk about God which is just the same as talk about ourselves (and therefore useless) and talk about him which has nothing to do with ourselves (and therefore meaningless). Words can be used neither univocally nor equivocally, to use the technical terms, but analogically. Certainly we may adopt this label, if we like, for our use of words as "pointers" to God's attributes, but it would be easy to suppose that some discussions of analogy are trying to *prove* something on the basis of a general principle.

I now turn to the question of God's governance of the world. Why, if he is omnipotent, does he allow so much evil in it? It is generally agreed that the apparent absence of any satisfactory answer to this question is the commonest reason for ruling God out from the start. So much has been and still is written about it that one might think it useless to take up the topic again. Certainly there is no simple solution which clears everything up, but I hold that the obscurities which have to be faced are no sufficient reason for abandoning belief in God. If there has been a definitive apprehension of him, that conclusion follows immediately. If there is *knowledge* of God (in the strong sense of which I have been speaking), anything which appears to contradict it cannot in fact do so. But there are very many people who would say that they believe in God but that they do not claim such knowledge. They have, perhaps, a strong "suspicion" of him, but the problem of evil threatens to stifle it. It may begin to look as if it *were* something which rules God out from the start. The "suspicion" may be wishful thinking or the result of one's training and so forth. From my point of view, the first thing to be said is that the "suspicion", even so, deserves to be followed up, and I have tried to explain how I think this has to be done. The evidence that it can be successfully followed up is abundant and strong. Wishful thinking and so forth is not, I should maintain, a plausible explanation of it. Nevertheless the problem of evil is there and has to be tackled.

I begin with moral evil. It seems to me that one can properly speak of a traditional Christian view of the matter; I refer not just to the views of Christian writers, although in these I think we do find a norm of Christian thinking about this, but to the Christian consciousness at large (that of the truly faithful, not that of merely nominal Christians), which has sometimes to be distinguished from the speculations of theologians. For me there is a Christian tradition, a faith once delivered to the saints, and I find bound up with it the conviction that man must choose God or reject him and the conviction that since God is the source of all good all evil is somehow the result of sin.

That is not to deny that there have been aberrations on these matters at certain periods even among devout Christians. I refer to the Christian tradition here because I want to say at once that the point of view which I shall be proposing may fail to win conviction unless it is seen in the context of this tradition, although it is, in my opinion, the most reasonable one apart from such considerations. That is, I am not saying that you have first to accept the Christian tradition if you are to make sense of it, but you may well begin with only a "suspicion" about it which the Christian tradition could confirm.

I also want to refer at the outset to certain approaches to the problem which enjoy some popularity at the present time. There is the pragmatic appeal—the suggestion that Christianity offers no theoretical solution to the problem but does something better by coping with it in practice, for it teaches us that God reconciles the world to himself in Christ. That simply evades the question of God's responsibility for the presence of evil which makes reconciliation a requirement. And there is also nowadays among Christians a recrudescence of the view, repudiated by the tradition, that a final rejection of God can never occur, for God sees to it that in the end everyone will be united with him. It is sometimes added that sin is inevitable, which contradicts what the tradition means by "sin", and that God uses evil as an indispensable means to our spiritual development, which clearly makes him directly responsible for it. (If it is said that God "permits" sin in view of a greater good which will be obtained thereby, doesn't this imply that he could always prevent it if he wished? And if that is the case, is it comprehensible that he should not so wish?) If the question of choosing God arises at all, does it make sense to suggest that this choice is never exercised by us in a fully developed form, that we are never faced with absolute alternatives but are always in a state in which our wills are fluctuating, neither turning definitively away from God nor turning definitively towards him? And if this does not make sense, if there must be sometime a definitive choice, how can God overturn it without destroying our freedom?

What we have to say, I believe, is this (let me repeat that to make sense of it you do not have to be a Christian). God, being supergenerous, creates a developing system which builds up entities of increasing subtlety and complexity and culminates in man (whether he also creates purely spiritual, non-bodily, beings is a question which will arise later). Such an arrangement commends itself to us, I suggest, as having a peculiar beauty. It and all its parts (in so far as we can regard them in isolation) are God's finite manifestation of himself. He loves it, unchangeably, timelessly, as such (it must be remembered that I am speaking of God's unique world, not a world which could have been left in a state of "possibility" in favour of some other). The "great chain of being" is commonly referred to in our time as a mediaeval notion with the implication that it is no longer thinkable. I cannot see that there is anything unthinkable about it in the form in which I am presenting it. Man, to continue, is capable of union with God : he can be aware of God and his awareness can grow; it is at risk, but it can become definitively established. It is this element of risk which makes moral evil possible—but we are now facing the fundamental difficulty, for it is by no means immediately obvious that this element can be reconciled with what we mean by God.

It seems to me that it can be in the following way. The definitive awareness of God cannot be, as it were, "laid on" from the start because it is impossible without love. Indeed the business of awareness is to grow into love, and that, for us, involves freedom of choice. (And if there is to be choice, there must be first the opportunity to choose : there must be contact with what is offered.) That a developing awareness is impossible without love is a theme which has been touched on already. We can fail to take any interest in the invasion of our experience by the Absolute; if we do it remains only a tiresome interruption, and for practical purposes we can get rid of it altogether. Moral evil lies in our refusal to follow the light. We receive the offer—there is a contact with God, and it produces at least a "suspicion" of him. But we shall not be in a full sense "aware" of him if we make no response to the offer. A personal act, one which involves our whole being, is required of us.

But this cannot mean that we contribute something from our own resources. We have no resources of our own. If what I have said about the source of existence is true, what I have now to say is that God will fill us with the knowledge and love of himself so that we can be completely his and he can be ours (two ways of saying the same thing) *provided that* we put no obstacle in his way. He *gives* us this "personal act" *if* we are willing to have it. He cannot give it to us if we are unwilling. Nor is this a denial of his omnipotence. To say that God is omnipotent is to say that he is the source of everything that comes *positively* to be. It is as our *good* that we find him in the first place, and all that we say about him must derive from our original experience. An abstract notion of "omnipotence" is not to the point. What is to the point is that the refusal in which moral evil lies is precisely *not* a positive contribution to the sum of things. When God is called the source of reality, then, this does not mean that he is the source or moral evil but precisely that he is *not*. But that again does not mean that moral evil is an illusion. It is a fact, a very mysterious one which we have to refer to in negative terms, and one for which we are responsible. It prevents things from coming to be. It does not diminish God, but it deprives us of what we should otherwise receive. It can make us incapable of receiving anything. It is so mysterious that I have sympathy with those who regard moral freedom as an illusion on that ground. But I claim that it is a fact of experience.

In stating what makes sense to me about the element of risk I may seem only to have made things more difficult. Our freedom, it will be objected, has been reduced to a power of refusal—in other respects we are puppets in God's hands. Even if a need for choice could be established, it would not explain why we should be subjected to so many and such appalling hazards. If God's generosity involves the risk of hell, it is, to put it mildly, a questionable sort of generosity.

I shall take these objections in order. When God gives us our "personal act" he does not just push us around like inanimate things; as we came into existence as living beings when he created us, giving us ourselves, so when he continues to act upon us we ourselves grow, and the "personal act" which he gives us is no less ours for being wholly derived from him. Why should people feel that the dignity of man is being impugned unless they think that man is in the strict sense creative, in which case God must be ruled out? Yet we find Christians saying that God "limits himself" or bestows some measure of his creative power on us. How can a Christian claim to be independent of God as an author of *good*? It is disconcerting enough to find that he is the author of moral evil. We may call it positive not indeed in the sense of a reality derived from God but in the sense that it is not only a fact but one which produces effects of the greatest moment. To refuse the good is to yield to the attractions of a policy which leads to disaster, to the rejection of other people's claims upon us, from which the worst horrors may follow. But it remains that moral evil itself lies in the refusal and the rejection. As such it must be called negative. God does put the future of the world in our hands by giving us our freedom. But there can be no question of his "changing his mind" and taking it back again. He creates a world-order which includes our freedom—it is unthinkable that we should be *forced* to love him. If we had not this mysterious power to refuse, should we not indeed be automata? And that we should have to grow up to our definitive choice is what we should expect in view of our origins —the risk is not needlessly complicated. But we have still to face the fundamental difficulty that it is the risk of total disaster.

To face it, then, at last, should we not after all declare God an illusion if the acceptance of him involves such a consequence? Could the God of whom I have been speaking make possible such a disaster? To say that he "takes a risk" might suggest that we can think of a God who *chooses* whether to create or not; on my view, if that language is used, it can only refer to the *fact* of his creating us as free to accept him, from which it follows that *we* are at risk. And what this means is that God has given us everything conceivable and that failure can result only from our own deliberate choice. How does this contradict what is claimed as our knowledge of him? It will be said that he "had no business" to create us when he knew that failure was not only possible but would in fact occur. And again, God, if we accept him as a hypothesis and for the purposes of argument, may not be faced, if you like, by alternative courses, but if he is the sort of person who can be approached by his creatures only at the hazard of eternal torments, then his credibility evaporates. The first move in this attack requires the reminder that God does not *foreknow* anything. He just sees things as they are. And he cannot see failure unless it is there to see. If it is there to see, there must be an existing creature to be responsible for it. Moreover the suggestion that he should contemplate creating somebody and then decide against it in view of its consequences brings us back to the supposal that he is faced by alternatives. The second move, which does not involve that supposal, puts the final issue starkly before us once more. It may be true that we cannot think of a beneficent God without allowing the possibility of a final failure, but is that not a reason for regarding him as unthinkable? If final failure does mean eternal torments, that is indeed difficult to answer. But are we obliged to think of it in those terms?

"Hell" means, for Christians, the loss of God. It seems, then, to involve the atrophy of man's spiritual powers. This is an appalling thought for those who appreciate their value, and that would explain in principle the lurid language which has been used about it. But what does it mean for those who are in that condition? Can we say more than that it is a sub-human condition? (We may add that we do not know whether any human being is in fact in it, but this does not justify us in disregarding the possibility of it.)

Accepting this proposal would not, of course, clear everything up. There is always the obscurity which surrounds both the life of God and our own moral freedom. It seems to me that we should accept the whole range of our experience, the summons of the infinite and our responsibility. It may fairly be asked what the alternative can be. For, to repeat, simply washing one's hands of the whole business is not a satisfactory one, since you cannot dismiss everything as *non*sense without implying (inconsistently) that something could make *sense*. If there is little or no interest in God, the problem of evil will often seem fatal to religion. If an interest is maintained, obscurity may yield ground to gratitude. It will not disappear, but it will be put in its proper place.

The problem, however, has a side to it on which I have hardly touched : there is physical as well as moral evil. The world's future, I have said, is put into our hands by God, who is not going to take away our freedom. If we choose wrongly, destructive effects will follow. And we cannot regard them as merely negative. When we reject the right course (what in this situation is the good) it seems that we must be pursuing nevertheless something which presents itself as a kind of self-fulfilment or at least as a means of avoiding harm. If we attended to the good, to the demands of the situation, we should abstain from actions which are seen to be harmful in ways which make them unjustifiable. If we withdraw our attention from the good, a competing interest takes control of us. I ought not to poison my creditor to save myself from ruin. But to save myself from ruin is a worthy enough object in itself. In creating us as free God gives us the power to choose between the good which the situation demands and our short-term private advantages. Our rejection of the good is not God's affair, but the pursuit of our well-being in whatever form must be empowered by him. There is something positive about all the changes which our actions produce. So if I say that God has created a world-order and that he is not going to change it, I must face the fact that he empowers us to positive action from which harmful effects often directly follow. He does not only give us a power of action and then leave it to us to use as we think fit. He must empower us *in* the use of it even when we cause harm, for he *gives* us *all* our activity. He is therefore responsible for physical evil in a sense in which he is not responsible for moral evil.

This conclusion may not seem to constitute a fresh problem, for we cannot conceive of a world-order in which God withdraws his empowering from us when we intend some short-term advantage from which evil will follow. But it does raise the problem of unjust suffering. What, in fact, do we mean by God's providence? I shall postpone an attempt to answer the general question until the next chapter when it will arise in the context of Christian theology.

Until God's plan for us has been envisaged in this larger framework we cannot pursue the subject much further. But there are two aspects of it on which something must be said before I end the present chapter. I have mooted the suggestion that physical evil must be explained as the consequence of moral evil, and it may well be asked how natural disasters, floods and so forth, can be accounted for in that way. There is also the special question of the suffering of animals who cannot share the compensations to which we may look forward.

It has often been held that natural disasters and the suffering that they bring are due to limitations inherent in a finite world. Things which have only a limited goodness are bound to get in one another's way. And there are some goods which cannot be had without evils. For example, there is the special enjoyment of relief when a distressing situation has come to an end. The example, however, does not seem to show that this state of mind possesses a special value; it is a matter of being restored to one's normal condition. To take another case, it *is* possible to love God as he ought to be loved without suffering a martyr's death. In general this approach to the problem envisages God as having to deal with intractable materials. Moral freedom, in my view, is intractable in the sense that the possibility of evil necessarily follows from it. But I do not see why we should say that there is anything else of this kind in a world which is God's created manifestation of himself—that is why I am disposed to conclude that physical evil must result from moral evil and from nothing else. It will be said that we have no business to regard natural phenomena as evils, but in so far as they cause undeserved or apparently needless suffering how can we fail to do so? The question, then, is whether we can regard the world of our present experience as the created showing-forth of God's absolute value. If it is not merely incomplete but also the scene of constant discords from which suffering results is it compatible with a genuine awareness of infinite super-generous activity? We can think of God's action upon the world, it seems to me, only as his unchanging beneficence which does everything for the good of his creatures in all the circumstances which their own shortcomings bring about. And it is clear that there are disorders in the world, natural phenomena from which suffering results, which are not due to the shortcomings of human beings.

The Christian tradition offers a possible explanation of these. (I am not saying that it is an essential element in that tradition, but it goes back a very long way.) It is one which encounters a good deal of prejudice today, for it postulates the existence of spiritual beings who do not fit into an exclusively evolutionary context. But there is no reason why the developing world of our experience should be all that there is of created reality. That there should be other non-bodily intelligent beings is not only conceivable but even probable. It seems to complete one's picture of created reality. The suggestion, then, is that the angels, who have the same destiny as ourselves, the same offer of God's love, did not all accept it—there was a fall of angels, and this led to a disturbance of our visible world, for the whole created system is bound up in all its parts or, to put it in traditional language, "the great chain of being" is affected throughout all its length. Whether God's beneficence is compatible with this dependence of his creatures on one another is a question which must be considered when I take up the topic of his providence. It must be enough to point out here that a Christian is entitled to appeal to it in answer to our present question.

Perhaps, some will say, you may succeed in satisfying yourself that there can be some sufficient explanation for the sufferings of human beings, but it is quite obvious that the sufferings of the other animals cannot be explained along the lines which you have been indicating. You may make some show of arguing that human suffering can be "worth while", but when it comes to the other animals you must admit complete defeat. There is, however, the question whether the other animals can be said to experience what we mean by suffering. It does indeed seem absurd at first sight to raise that question. But there are certain facts which have to be faced, however disconcerting to our natural assumptions they may be. We are assured on good authority that human beings who have received an anaesthetic, preventing pain but not abolishing all consciousness, have shown all the signs of pain, struggling when they were struck on sensitive spots, but afterwards denying categorically that they had *suffered*. If this is indeed the case, we can only conclude that what we mean by suffering pain requires the full exercise of the specifically human power which I have called "awareness". A reflective power which we normally exercise was inhibited by the anaesthetic. If, as I proposed in the first chapter, the other animals have a life of sensation and do not share our awareness at all, then they react to interference as sensitive physical organisms, but they do not feel what *we mean* by "pain".

This has been a very sketchy discussion. But it will have served its purpose if it has shown reason for thinking that the claims of theism cannot be dismissed out of hand, that the difficulties which it has to face are at least not obviously insuperable, and that the hypothesis of a self-revelation of the Absolute in Jesus Christ is not therefore without interest. In the next chapter I shall consider on what conditions that hypothesis could be verified.

Just as "belief in God' can have a weak sense in which it means a commitment based on evidence which is less than conclusive and a strong sense in which it means a definite awareness and acceptance of him, so it is with belief in Christ. I have mentioned already the confirmation which belief in God (in the weak sense) can receive from the discovery of him in Christ, but that discovery too may be something less than definite. There may be just a growing interest in Christianity, strengthening an original "suspicion" of God, which leads to the decision to accept it as a working hypothesis. From the point of view of traditional Christian theology, this will normally issue in the definite awareness and acceptance of God's revelation of himself in Christ, which may indeed be expected to occur without the need for a previous experimental stage. And that is what it means to have Christian *faith*. The present climate of thought has led many people, among them Christian theologians of a generally orthodox kind, to talk as though faitn could never be more than a working hypothesis. It is, of course, always at risk. It is often subjected to the severest trials. But it can be proof against such trials. Can anyone suppose that the New Testament writers (not to mention witnesses of later times) are fairly described as having committed themselves to nothing more than a working hypothesis? I propose to speak of the gift of faith as something which has, of its nature, the power to give us certainty, although it can exercise its influence on us in an initial, incomplete, way. An exaggerated view that it must exercise its power either completely or not at all has promoted an exaggerated reaction to the other extreme—a denial that it is faith's proper business to give us certainty at all.

But does the acceptance of Christianity presuppose even a "suspicion" of God? In practice it might seem that often enough people make their first contact with him when the Gospel is preached to them. But if I am right to say that we are in fact in contact with him whenever we are *obedient to the truth,* then we can hardly suppose that this has not happened before there has been any "hearing of the Word". But it may well be that God is first *recognised* in Christ. Moreover, to be convinced that Christ is God's messenger requires, so I shall argue, that we must have God's own guarantee that this is so; we must somehow hear God speaking to us about it; and so we must first (logically) satisfy ourselves that it is *God* who is speaking. Only on these conditions, it seems to me, can it be claimed that the gift of faith has the *power* to give us certainty.

That is an account of faith which is still unfamiliar in many quarters as a result of that attitude of suspicion, to which I referred earlier, in regard to all claims to a direct (though not immediate) awareness of God. The theological revival of our time is restoring it to currency. It is becoming recognised that unless there is an *experience* of God as the Father of Jesus Christ or, to put it in other words, an experience of Jesus as speaking with the voice of God, the claims made for faith cannot be intellectually justified. What, then, is to be said to the many professing Christians who do not claim that sort of faith but regard God's revelation of himself in Christ as at most highly probable? They will sometimes say that the Christian message gives them hope, but not certainty. They would be wrong, they feel, to abandon this hope, and it may be called, if you like, some kind of experience. But it is an experience which does not banish all doubts about the truth of Christianity. The first thing to say, perhaps, is that it is not yet a question of how much is implied by the acceptance of Christ as God's messenger (when people speak of "the truth of Christianity" they are sometimes thinking of particular doctrines which may not in fact prove to be bound up with it—or rather perhaps not in the form which they have in mind). But the most important consideration for such people is surely that there have been (and are) those whose experience does seem to have taken them all the way. Can we suppose that a man like Saint John of the Cross, for example, was suffering all the time from hallucinations? One's answer may still be hesitating, but if that sort of faith begins to seem *probably* genuine in particular instances it becomes easier to believe that one's own could move in that direction. Indeed some people, thinking along these lines, have found that after all they themselves were certain already, that beneath all the puzzles and obscurities there *was* something solid and immovable. At least it is fair to ask that the possibilities of faith should not be decided upon until the field of enquiry has been properly investigated.

What I am proposing, in accordance with the tradition, is that faith is the "the seed of glory" and so the seed of mysticism : it must therefore itself have a mystical character. It must involve a sort of *seeing*. Mysticism, in this sense, is not something reserved for extraordinary people. That is likely to appear quite implausible at first and will need a good deal of explaining. I want to begin by

saying something about certain accounts of faith which are probably much more familiar. Books of Christian apologetics are easy
to find (although perhaps no longer being written) which give the
impression that one must first have definite evidence which reveals
the *fact* of revelation, a logical *proof* that a supernatural event has
actually occurred, before one can go on to have *faith* in the revelation—that being understood to mean an entire trust in it and so the
acceptance in advance of such truths as it may prove to declare to
us. This is not the language in which the Gospels or the earlier
centuries of Christianity talked about faith, and the objections
which it provokes are pretty obvious. It may be difficult to account
for the rise of Christianity unless we suppose that something "supernatural" had occurred (it seems to me, indeed, extremely difficult
to find an alternative explanation for so many extraordinary facts),
but it must be acknowledged that there are various theories which
could conceivably provide explanations. It cannot be said that we
are *forced* to accept a supernatural explanation by the sheer weight
of the historical evidence. How could facts accessible to the
historian provide conclusive evidence of any "supernatural" happening? Moreover, if we suppose for the sake of argument that a
coercive proof of this kind *were* available, it would mean that faith
could result automatically from the exercise of our reasoning
powers alone. Trusting in the revelation would not make any difference to this state of affairs, because if once you have proved
that God is speaking it would be simply absurd to suppose that he
was deceiving you. All Christians must agree that faith cannot be
forced on anyone. Belief in Christ is, of its nature, *refusable*.

It might be said that the evidence is capable of producing conviction but that people run away from it without giving themselves
time to examine it properly because they fear the consequences of
accepting it. But the freedom which is claimed for faith does not
mean a freedom to draw back before the evidence is complete. It
is the freedom to accept a gift when that is definitively offered. To
understand this it has to be remembered that religious knowledge
cannot develop without love. We can be aware of God as summon-
ing us in the context of the Christian message. This is itself a
knowledge of him. But it is only a first stage. We have to respond
to it by keeping our attention on it—that is, we are free not to do
so. If we do keep our attention on it (in other words, if we give
ourselves to it, and this is what love means) then—but only on this
condition—God gives us that *fuller* knowledge of himself which is

the gift of faith. We enter into that personal relationship with him which is the life of grace. This must be what always happens whenever anyone gives himself to God, whether or not this happens in conscious response to the Gospel message. This must be the meaning of "baptism by desire", and so this was what the first two chapters of this book were really all about. And the transition to the life of grace must be the meaning of the *supernatural* character which faith is said to possess. But all this, someone might say, is dodging the question. Faith could be free in the sense just explained, but we are asking whether we are free to accept the fact of revelation, and if we are aware of God's summons in hearing the Gospel have we not found ourselves informed of it thereby? We have not *chosen* to accept this fact. I should reply that the question which ought to be asked is whether or not we are free to choose God *in* his revelation. It may be added that, if we reject his summons (if we turn our attention from it), we *are* rejecting "the fact of revelation" and may succeed in forgetting the whole business.

Although some zealous apologists may have seemed to say that it is all just a question of studying the historical evidence, in fact this sort of apologist does grant, if pressed, that such evidence is not itself conclusive. But this admission has often led to a most unsatisfactory account of the supernatural character of faith. It is suggested that God enables us "supernaturally" to accept what the historical evidence cannot of itself convincingly demonstrate by arousing in us the desire for eternal life, promised to us as the reward of faith, and by strengthening our willingness to commit ourselves to a hazard. Somehow he gives us the assurance that we are in the right way. There are various versions of this story, but they agree in saying that God's empowering of us is in the first instance an empowering of the *will,* which is then supposed to have repercussions upon the intellect. Such accounts are concerned to avoid a justification of faith in terms of fresh evidence, over and above the historical facts. God makes us certain that the evidence is sound, but he does not present himself to the *mind* in doing so. But how can we have God's authority for revelation, unless we *find* him as authorising it? We must be "in touch" with him as somehow declaring to us that Jesus Christ is indeed his beloved Son. We must be aware of him as issuing an invitation to accept his Son, in and through whom we can enter into the supernatural relationship with him. Intellect and will are indeed closely bound up with one another, as the theory which I have been criticising insists, but not in the way that it proposes, for there must first be awareness before the will can be engaged. Faith is not a kind of "wishful thinking"; it must be established on the solid intellectual basis of an awareness of God as the revealer.

To sum up this issue, if the evidence available to our minds is itself insufficient, there can be no justification for committing ourselves absolutely to it. And it is certainly part of the Christian tradition that faith has the power to provide us with such justification, even though, so I have suggested, it may not always provide it in particular circumstances (that is, when it has only *begun* to do its work in us, not only difficulties but also real doubts may remain). At the back of the theories which I have criticised is the assumption that no direct awareness of God is possible for us; it is not understood that such an awareness can be a mediated one. It is this that has led to the suggestion God can ("supernaturally") make us certain of what we can in no way *see*. If Christian faith makes sense, it must carry with it some sort of *vision*. Nor can talk of the "supernatural" make sense except on that condition. This is the conclusion to which theologians are returning. I must now face the question : *what* sort of vision is it?

In so far as it is an awareness of God it is (strictly) indescribable. To make a further attempt to talk round it, it has that character of absoluteness or finality which always attaches to knowledge of *God* and also that of precariousness and incompleteness which attaches to all our knowledge as *ours*. It has, except in very special cases, the same sort of obscurity as it has in other circumstances, all knowledge of God being mediated, whether just by our own self-awareness or also by our contemplation of Jesus Christ in whom his Father is manifested to us (for although the Father must accredit him to us if we are to accept him as the Son, it is *in* the Son that we are united with him in the knowledge of faith). The impact made upon men by Christ's human life can, however, be described. The writers of the Gospels describe it. He seems to be both like other men and yet also in certain ways unlike them. We find in him a more complete fulfilment of our own aspirations than we find in anyone else. I am not saying that this difference is inevitably perceived by all readers of the Gospel, but that it is there to be perceived. It may not reveal that special status which Christians attribute to Jesus Christ, his unique relationship with the Father, but it does mark him out in some way. His difference from other men may seem to the reader only a difference of degree. But it seems right to say that the story of the Gospels does appear to the unprejudiced reader a story with features that are unique. This is where the journey to faith may begin. The experience of the first Christians is described to us, and it exercises an attraction. God's summons to the Christian life, I shall say, is beginning to make itself heard.

But it is possible for a man to realise that Christians of his acquaintance have something special about them even before he has taken any interest in the Gospels. The life of Christ which he communicates to his followers can shine through them (whether in fact it often does so is irrelevant here), as the beauty of God can shine through the beauty of the created world. But a man may not *recognise* that this is indeed the life of Christ, just as he may not *recognise* that what shines through the world is God's beauty. In either case he is "in touch" with God—it is *God* who is "before his mind"—and if he accepts what he finds as absolute he has the "grace" of God. Christians believe that Christ is always in fact the mediator of grace even when a man accepts the Absolute with no knowledge at all of Christianity. But in the case which I am considering there is a conscious contact with a power which is Christ's, although recognised so far only as "something special" about Christians. This man finds God acting in them in a special way, even though perhaps he may not as yet use the language of God about it. Then he may turn to the Gospels and discover eventually what it really is that he has found. If he has already accepted as absolute what he has found in Christians he will have been already "in touch" with the new life which Christ has brought into the world. He has much more to learn, but he has already listened to God's Word.

How has this come about? How can one see what is happening in the depths of another's experience and transfer it to one's own? One could reach the conclusion that "there must be something in it", and one might then be *told about* it. But that would not be the same as *having* this experience. If the journey to faith begins in this way, it can end only in an experience of one's own, a summons to oneself. Contact with Christians would thus be the occasion, the natural preparation, for one's own hearing of the Word. God has not left himself without witness in the world at any time. But in "the fullness of time" he offers "the fullness of life" to men *through* men, through and in Christ "in whom dwells all the fullness of the Godhead bodily" and through those to whom Christ communicates his life, whether in the first instance they are met with in the Gospels or elsewhere—but through them on those occasions only in the sense that they lead those who meet them to look in the right direction. What they have in some sense to *see* is this indwelling of the Godhead in Christ. God reveals Christ to them as the Son so that in the Son they may find him as the Father. It must be left to the next chapter to consider how this relationship of Son to Father is to be understood. But it may be added here, now that God's approach to us through other men has been touched on, that according to Christian belief, although God's grace is available for all men, this new life of the Christian dispensation can be found in its fullness only in membership of the society of Christians. As it is often put today, that forms the "spearhead" of Christ's peaceful penetration into human society at large.

All this should be providing materials for an answer to the question : what *sort* of vision does faith involve? It may not seem to be a vision at all. It is the awareness of a power which one cannot rightly resist, the recognition of God's love as inviting us to receive it as it overflows from a heart which is open to it as no other heart has ever been or will be—not, of course, that we must at first express it to ourselves like that, but this is what we can recognise that it has always been. At first perhaps we would only say that the promise of fulfilment is somehow held out to us unambiguously in the Christian Church. Perhaps the unreflecting Christian could only say that in some mysterious fashion he feels *bound* to the Church. But if he has indeed the assurance of faith, it must be God's work in him— it must be God's testimony to the truth of Christianity, a direct awareness of him as the Revealer. In a man's early years he may have taken it all for granted. When he has to ask himself whether he *does* believe, it will not be until his merely human props prove to be insufficient that he discovers what faith really is.

It is the attitude of loving attention to Christ, recognised as the definitive manifestation of God's love for us. People may merely shrug their shoulders at the suggestion that such an attitude can be honestly adopted by an intelligent man. This is, they may say, much too good to be true. An awareness of God sounds fantastic enough, but an announcement of this kind which he is supposed to make in the depths of one's soul about a shadowy figure in the distant past —that is completely absurd. Until the curiosity of these critics can be aroused in a more than merely casual way, a Christian cannot expect to make an impression on them. And if their curiosity has not been so aroused, he must ask himself whether *he* is to blame for it. Something can be said, however, to make clearer what is meant by God's testimony to his Son. He does not direct the mind to the past, bringing before it a man who once lived in Palestine and providing in some sort of telepathic way the requisite information about him. It is the risen Christ who presents himself to us, positively though still obscurely, when the journey to faith reaches the point of crisis (if we are going to talk about a "proof" of his resurrection, it is this, not the evidence for an empty tomb, strong though that is). He has run his own course to the bitter end and his human powers have received the fulfilment which could be obtained only in the transition from this life to the next. To say that God reveals him to us is to say that we find him with these powers. In them we find *God's* power at work; we have his guarantee that this man is *his* in a new and definitive way. Christ is "the power and the wisdom of God", and so he can be himself directly present to us. The *fullness* of his presence is found in the Church (which is the same, as I shall try to explain later, as saying "in the Eucharist"). But he has now the freedom to make contact with us as the incarnate Son, risen and "glorified", whenever we can be brought to open our minds to him—he does not *force* himself upon us, and we must be in some sense prepared for his coming.

That is what must be more fully discussed. The Apostles received the revelation directly from him. So, in the last analysis, does everyone. But the experience of the Apostles became the medium in which it was revealed to those who followed them, and *their* successors received it likewise, whether by word of mouth or by reading the accounts of the Apostles' experience in the Gospels. That God should make such dispositions does not seem to me at all surprising. An intimate acquaintance with the text of the bible is not required for faith. A most ardent faith can spring up on the basis of a very small amount of information. The only essential information seems to have been contained, for the first Christians, in the statement that Christ is the Lord. What is required for faith is entering into the life of the Church, the life of Christ which he shares with it. The more fully we enter into it, the more ardent our faith will be. That requires from us pre-eminently attention and love, that is to say, prayer and that many-sided work for the kingdom of God which is also prayer. The study of the bible in the light of faith is the food of prayer, and it can also be work for the kingdom of God in a peculiarly important way. But without faith it will not reveal the message. The Gospel, the message enshrined in the New Testament writings, is preached in and by the Church. Without it Christ would be unknown. *In* it he presents himself for our faith and in him we find the power of God who authenticates the message. By the same token he authenticates the Church's experience. (The unfolding of it into theology will be the topic of the following chapter.)

These, I believe, are the conditions on which faith's assurance is justified. But what will the biblical critics say about it, and the professors of comparative religion and other learned persons? Are we not short-circuiting their problems? It must be very provoking for scholarly researchers, scrupulously concerned not to exaggerate their evidence, when these tremendous conclusions are reached by the unlearned on the basis, apparently, only of the wildest hypotheses. But I have been trying to show that this is not the case. Faith is not a hypothesis but the acceptance of evidence not available to the scholar considered simply as such. Its claim is an extremely startling one for the non-Christian, who indeed may be in all honesty quite bewildered by such extravagant statements on the lips of sane men, and a Christian should expect this reaction. But it is not a claim which scholars could upset unless it could be proved that the Jesus of history did *not* have the special relation to God which is claimed for him by faith or that Christianity had no founder at all but was somehow invented by the first Christian community. It does not appear how either of these negative conclusions could be established. But suppose it could be shown that Jesus himself made no claims to special status (that the claims were a later invention), would that not be at least very awkward for the man of faith? To all such questions he has to repeat that he has his own evidence—which means that it will not be contradicted.

There is no reason why there should be clashes between Christian and non-Christian students of the bible. That is, both parties can approach the evidence simply as scholars and reach the same sort of conclusions. The Christian, however, reading the bible in the light of the revelation, will see in it what the non-Christian does not see. He needs to be careful not to allow this to interfere with his purely scholarly judgements. If he tried to resist the conclusions of non-Christian scholars on the ground that they were ruled out by faith, he would betray an incomprehension not only of scholarship and the claims of truth but also of faith itself. When interference with scholars has occurred, it has often been due to exaggerated claims for faith. It has been supposed that the evidence of faith must imply doctrines which are not in fact part of revelation but theological *theories* or assumptions, and Christian scholars have been attacked for concluding that the message of the New Testament is incompatible with them. Here it must be emphasised that Christian experience, although rooted in the message found in the New Testament, can see further and further *into it* in virtue of a contact with the same revelatory power which aroused the faith of the first Christians. Scripture and "tradition" are the fruits of the same developing experience.

Nor can the claim to a definitive revelation contradict, or be contradicted by, historical findings in any field of enquiry. In every case the same principles apply. This claim is no denial that God has enlightened the founders of other religious movements or that other religious traditions have their value. But in an obvious sense any claim to truth is exclusive. Again, such a claim, for many minds, will seem bewilderingly extravagant, and this is what the Christian must expect.

At this point I want to return to the topic of God's providence now that we have a fuller context for it. What difference does belief in Christ make to the problems which this topic raises for us? In the first place it makes our life gain enormously in value, for, when God's grace is recognised for what it is, a union with him in Christ, we gain an understanding of its possibilities for us which we cannot otherwise have. And we are more ready to acknowledge, with Saint Paul, that the sufferings of the present time are not worthy to be compared with the glory that shall be revealed in us. It becomes easier to realise that God's generosity is unlimited. The power to overcome the evil in ourselves, when it can be recognised and drawn upon as the power which Christ gives us, emphasises this generosity for us. We are less likely to slip back into the despairing conclusion that the difficulties of life are not worth while—to think, that is, that our state is not, after all, worthy of the God in whom we believed.

But this suggests another difficulty. God is being generous to us, we may feel, but what about all those who have had no chance of benefiting by the coming of Christ? It may be said that they will do so in the end, that the same destiny is prepared for everyone, but they certainly did not enjoy our present advantages. That leads to the consideration that a developing world which finds its supreme point in Christ (an arrangement which cannot be thought

55

unworthy of God) must inevitably lead to inequalities—not that anyone can fail to achieve his fulfilment save through his own deliberate rejection of it, but in the sense that he will make his ineluctable choice in conditions which will present him with these or those difficulties which people in other circumstances are spared. It would not be reasonable to complain of this. And it leads to the further consideration that God deals with us not as isolated individuals but as members of the human race. We each have a particular part to play in the development of a vast society on which we depend in innumerable ways and which in turn depends, in however small a measure, on us. God's providence regards us as such.

It is only when we look at things like this, perhaps, that we can face up to the fact that God puts the future of the world in our hands with results that tempt us to cry out against injustice—and so to reject him (but even so a commitment to the claims of justice *will* be belief in him). For we must say, I think, that God's beneficence does not just put us as individuals in a state of inevitable risk, the risk that we may as individuals reject his love—it puts us also at risk in that as members of our race we may hinder instead of helping one another. What we have to say, then, is that God makes his offer to us as individuals in a society, giving us the power to help one another—that is what the society is *for*—but a power which is inevitably at risk because as individuals, summoned to God's love, we cannot be constrained in our use of it. The higher the stakes, the greater is the danger. What would be unworthy of God would be putting the stakes lower, supposing that this were conceivable (for again it does not seem reasonable to complain when we cannot in fact conceive of some more comfortable and equally valuable set-up). What God gives us, if we are willing to take it, is the value of human society, the value of our love for one another, and it is this value in infinite form which the Christian revelation leads us to discover in the life of the Triune God.

All this may help to throw light on the way in which we may regard our human history. The events in it are (so I have suggested earlier) the meeting-points of God's super-generous unchanging beneficence and our freedom to reject it. The good which he offers us is always the good for *this* situation, distorted as it always is from the ideal, the situation in which we should be if there had been no sin in the world. This may perhaps be brought out by the suggestion made by Maurice Blondel (in *Cahier XXIV* of *La*

Nouvelle Journée) that the original scheme of salvation was willed by God in such a way that it would be *a priori* adaptable to the various eventualities which the very fact of created, fallible liberty makes possible. I have only to add that this was no arbitrary arrangement. When we realise that what God intends is always the good of all his creatures, that the good for one will conflict with the good of another, that it is the whole situation of a sinful world upon which at every moment his activity is directed and that there is no question of his abolishing the existing world-order, then we may realise that we cannot expect to follow the workings of his providence. We may also realise that he is not an automaton but is infinitely resourceful. The image of the sun in Plato's *Republic* is the basic one, perhaps, but it has to be corrected by others. I have given these conclusions bluntly in the endeavour to make them as clear as possible, but I am not, of course, suggesting that this is the last word on such profound matters.

By way of preparation for considering, in the next chapter, the development of the Christian experience into its central doctrines, I propose to face certain obstacles, which might seem to bar the way : the problems of original sin and of "predestination". The doctrine of original sin is not a central one; it arises in connection with the central doctrine of the Redemption, the doctrine that we can be brought to God only through Christ. But it has loomed very largely in theological discussion, and such disconcerting things have been said about it that it can arouse prejudice against all Christian theology. So here I shall offer a view of it which should not be disconcerting. Before broaching the question of *how* we are saved, it is desirable at least to exclude certain views about what we are saved *from*. In so far as "predestination" is a doctrine at all, it is the statement that God is the source of all good, and I shall say nothing further about that. But I should like to propose that the theological quarrels to which it has given rise are quarrels about the *philosophical* questions which I have just been discussing in so far as they have seemed to contradict God's omnipotence or else to deny our own freedom. Christians themselves, faced by these questions, have so often taken refuge, illegitimately, in "mystery", acknowledging in effect that we can see no way of escape from contradiction, although of course it is different for God. This is a fatal move. It makes our own powers of thought seem radically untrustworthy and it leads to the conclusion that, if we speak of God, we do not know at all of whom we are speaking. If God's ways are not our ways in the sense which is being implied, then he does indeed die "the death of a thousand qualifications", as some of our contemporaries like to put it. And this illegitimate appeal to "mystery" is another thing which can arouse prejudice against all Christian theology. Something, therefore, needs to be said about each of these rebarbative topics.

Original sin, in the language of theology, does not mean primarily the first sin ever committed but rather that *need* for God's grace which every human being brings with him into the world. Without God's grace we cannot attain him, and so this situation is not unnaturally painted in very sombre colours. But what is being described is in fact a lack and a privation, not a state of total corruption, for in that case human nature would be *deaf* to God's word. And such a state of affairs would indeed be incompatible with his love. There is a privation as well as a lack for this reason at least that we come into the world with a human nature tarnished by the sins of our ancestors. There are tendencies to evil in us which result from our heredity. We are members of a race which has failed in so many ways. The world into which we enter is full of unwholesome influences. There are temptations to face for whose existence others are responsible (we are responsible only in so far as we give way to them, and I have been trying to show that this state of things is not incompatible with God's love). Some theologians of our time suggest that these influences (which they often refer to as "the sin of the world") may be really all that we have to consider when we talk of the effects of original sin—we are deprived of a state in which these drawbacks would not be present. Is this consonant with the Christian tradition? These theologians suggest that it may be. Other theologians would hold that it is not, for according to the tradition we are deprived also of grace and it is that deprivation in which original sin essentially consists. That is, there was an *original grace,* a grace received by men at the beginning of our history, which was subsequently lost altogether, and it is available to us again through Christ alone. It is not necessarily bound up with this view that this grace was lost by us through the sin of a first human pair. Already we may draw a first conclusion that the doctrine of original sin is a very much vaguer affair than it has been commonly thought to be.

The loss of an original grace might suggest that the human race had cut itself off from God altogether. But perhaps it can be explained in the following way. There was in the beginning, let us suppose, the offer, made and accepted, of an intimacy with God which in the state of innocence would have been enjoyed by all members of the human family. When this was lost (and this could have resulted from a gradual process of deterioration whereby human nature was no longer the necessary substructure for it) we do not need to suppose—indeed we cannot suppose—that God consigned the race, apart from certain Old Testament characters, to general perdition. That, it must be frankly acknowledged, is what a good many Christians have at least appeared to be saying. God wills always that we should all be saved. "Grace" must always be available, even if original grace has been lost. It is this original grace—with which we may identify what theologians call "sanctifying grace"—which is restored by Christ. It is now something *new*, at least in so far as it is a fresh outpouring of "sanctifying grace"; most Christians today, perhaps, would hold that it was not just a restoring of it but the definitive gift for which the whole world-process was building up and which becomes available for us only through Christ's victory. The grace which was available even after "the fall" may be called "justifying grace". Those who received it are destined to that union with God in Christ which is his unchanging purpose for us, but not in their lifetime on this earth. Christians have already the privilege of entering upon it; they have a foretaste of the final union. This is the sort of inequality which is consonant with God's justice or is rather a sign of his unrestricted love, and so the doctrine of original sin should not be regarded as a barrier preventing us from all further advance.

"Predestination", too, constitutes no such barrier once it is accepted that our *refusal* to go forward does not itself involve God in any way. For the great dispute of the sixteenth and seventeenth centuries, left unsettled by the authorities of the Church, reduces to the question whether the loss of God requires his own refusal to give us grace. It may indeed seem strange that this question should have been raised, and theologians of our time are not much interested in it. Those who discuss it, I think one may say, more and more agree that the trouble arose from purely abstract theories about God's omnipotence. One side urged that unless he controls our actions, in the sense that he causes us to do what we do, then we shall be encroaching on his power, but it was not realised that this is true only of what we *positively* do—not of those refusals which, though real, are *negations*. I have already discussed this at some length. The other side urged that we have a *positive* freedom in a sense which (in effect) requires us to share God's own creative power. And the result was inevitably a deadlock. It is a pity that theologians do not take more trouble to dissipate the impression that this is an insoluble problem. Why not say fearlessly that it *is* for us to decide whether God's grace is to be "efficacious" or not? It is no restriction on God that he cannot force us to love. It is meaningless to suggest that he can. It is impious to make him directly responsible for sin. And no fresh difficulty arises from the contention that God has to "wait upon" our refusals. He is timelessly aware of them and therefore they do not change him. They cannot take anything from him. These are problems of theism, which has indeed its difficulties; but they are not special to Christian theology.

The total corruption of man's powers of thought and will, together with doctrines about God which make him seem arbitrary and even cruel—this is what is often thought to characterise the theology of the Reform. And the Catholic position is often thought to involve the sort of distinction between "nature" and "the supernatural" which makes grace in effect unnecessary for man. When this crude opposition is supposed to exist between Catholics and Protestants, there will be an unwillingness to consider Christian theology at all. Here is another barrier which I ought to face before ending this chapter. One of the most promising features, it seems to me, of today's situation is that Protestant and Catholic thinkers have been coming to realise that they have often been driven into extreme positions by reacting against one another. In a time of general upheaval it is not surprising that many cease, in effect, to be Christians and become secular humanists instead. But those whose faith has been purified by the upheaval find themselves drawing closer and closer together. For example, there are a good many friends of mine, not of the Roman communion but of various others, who do not therefore share my own convictions about the function of the Papacy (although even here we are closer than we were), but whose faith in the Christian revelation I joyfully recognise as being in all fundamental respects the same as my own. Our principles of thought and our fundamental beliefs seem to be just the same. And I believe that very many others are having this most encouraging experience. There is such a thing as the Christian tradition, and those of us who indeed have *faith* in Christ are coming more and more to understand one another as belonging to it.

To illustrate this very briefly, we all acknowledge our complete dependence upon God, even though we may not always agree when we philosophise about our moral freedom. Without God, we are impotent—it is his work in us which unites us with him. Some will say that without his grace we can register only his absence—we are under the Law, not under the Gospel. It seems to me that the awareness of God's absence must imply a contact with him. This I call a "natural knowledge" of God, an expression which is repugnant to so many Protestant thinkers. But it does not mean that we can "think up" God independently of him. It is his gift to us. All knowledge of God is in this sense his revelation to us. And this "natural knowledge" is not a state in which we can rest. It is the offer of God's definitive gift to us, the knowledge and love of him in Christ. Until we accept it we are indeed without the indispensable means of our salvation. And to accept it we must recognise our need for it and those tendencies within us which can draw us away from it. But again it seems to me that it is God's approach to us which makes us recognise our need. It may be our helplessness which moves us to throw ourselves upon him, but it is also the medium in which he makes contact with us. It is, I think, one and the same situation which is being experienced by people who describe it with different emphases and in different terminologies. Now at last we can turn to the content of the Christian experience. What have Christians found by exploring it?

To write only a single chapter on the unfolding of the Christian experience would be absurd in a work of general apologetics. But this book, although it has an apologetic purpose, has a strictly limited one, that of proposing a certain point of view about a "mystical element" in Christianity in a way which is intended to make the whole business seem more comprehensible. I have been concerned so far to suggest that both theism and faith in Christ are thinkable—on condition that a directness or "mystical element" is recognised as present in all awareness of God, and I must now try to show that, with this condition still in force, the central doctrines of Christianity can become intelligible. And I shall be concerned with them principally with a view to freeing them from that appearance of absurdity which they present to so many minds today; there can be no question of expounding them in any detail; moreover I shall have to take it for granted that Christianity *is* an affair of tradition (if it were not, it would not seem to have much claim on one's attention) and that these central doctrines have emerged in fact from the Christian experience.

First, what is the meaning of the basic claim that in Christ God was made man? Saint Thomas Aquinas, in the sixteenth question of the *Tertia Pars* (a. 6, ad 2), gives the traditional answer as follows : "When it is said 'God became man', no change on God's side is meant, but only on the side of human nature." The Council of Chalcedon had declared that there are two natures in Christ, the divine and the human, and that there is no confusion between the two. This doctrine is the subject of vigorous debate among Christians at the present time. How can it be reconciled with the unity of Christ's person which is certainly an essential datum of faith? How are we to avoid a swallowing up of the humanity in the divinity or of the divinity in the humanity? Let us first consider an answer which has been accepted in recent years by a number of theologians, Catholic as well as Protestant. This takes its stand on the Johannine formula "the word became flesh" and insists that we must take it quite literally. God, it is said, remains immutable "in himself", yet he can come to be "in the other". This statement has been frequently repeated with approval, but so far as I can see no light has been shed on it. It is surprising to me that it has provoked so far very little disapproval, although there are now signs that opposition to it is growing. It has been observed, for instance, that if there is said to be change in God at all, to suppose that God has an "inner being" which is immune from change seems to make no sense. That, it seems to me, is obvious. But let us see how the proposal is supported. We are told that we must be guided in our thought by the Christian revelation. This tells us *how* we should understand God's changelessness; it tells us that we must not regard it as incompatible with his *becoming* something. Indeed, if he could not, he would be lacking something. And after all God is always inexpressible. We can only "point to" him in words which can never exhaust our meaning. We can speak of him only "dialectically". When we say that he is "changeless", we must at once add the correction that he is nevertheless not "static". God's "changelessness" cannot mean that he has no real relations with his creatures. It is the Christian faith that, since Jesus Christ moved from place to place, *God* moved from place to place.

These statements are all to be found in the writings of contemporary, highly respected, theologians. What are we to make of them? In the first place it is to be observed that this view is not based on a philosophical theory about a developing God but upon the supposed requirements of the theological tradition which set it in opposition to what I would call our metaphysical experience. By our "metaphysical experience" I mean that awareness of the Absolute as infinite with which the first two chapters of this book were concerned. It is "natural" in that it is available, in principle, to everyone, but when it is freely entered into it becomes "supernatural". We must call it a revelation of God. And it is my contention that it reveals him to us as free from all imperfections, all limitations and all incompleteness. It is to the Absolute as "pointed to" like this that we find ourselves summoned. That, I shall say, is the fundamental datum of the religious consciousness. We are being asked to believe that the Christian revelation contradicts it, and this, if I am right, would mean the end of Christianity. It will be said that Christianity is not "a religion"—it is just the one definitive revelation of God. That is, we are being asked to acknowledge a new meaning for "God" which does not build on our human experience but replaces it with something incompatible with it. This seems to me to set up a barrier of incomprehensibility at the entrance of Christian theology. We are being asked to say that God abandons his absoluteness in the Incarnation and that this is to be considered an added perfection for him. I submit that this makes no sense. It is true that we must speak of God "dialectically"—to say that he is "changeless" must be understood in a positive sense so that we have to add at once that he is also "active", and this too is only a "pointer" to what we mean. But what we mean does exclude change absolutely. To say that we must hold together "change" and "changelessness" in God seems to me quite meaningless.

The supporters of the view which I am venturing to criticise, when they appeal to the "real relations" which God has with his creatures, are proposing that God must change because he is the creator, the source of all created reality. He changes in all his dealings with us, so that the Incarnation presents us in this respect with an instance of a general rule. The First Vatican Council, it is pointed out, did indeed declare that God is immutable but also declared that he is free in creating—and that means that he would have been different if he had chosen not to create. The act of creation, then, makes a difference to him, and so does all the activity which he directs upon his creatures. I have proposed that we can think of God's freedom in a way which does not subject him to change. There is no question, I have urged, of God's *not* creating. His activity directed upon the created universe, his finite but unique self-manifestation, is a timeless, changeless activity. It seems to me very strange to suggest that the First Vatican Council can be interpreted as meaning that God is immutable only in a "dialectical" sense which is compatible with his changing in regard to his creatures. It is surely much more sensible to interpret its saying that creation is "free' in a sense which is compatible with God's *not choosing* and to suppose that when it declared God immutable it meant what it said. Our theology has emerged from a period in which God's transcendence was constantly asserted but commonly thought of in abstract terms and at second-hand, a truth to be learned but not lived. The reaction against this is part of the present theological revival. But like all such reactions is is exposed to the danger of flying to the other extreme. God's transcendence, as discussed in the textbooks, had come to seem meaningless, and there is now the danger that giving it a new look may lead to abolishing it altogether.

When we are told that God moved from place to place because Jesus Christ who did so *is* God, it might seem sufficient to say that the divine and the human natures are being confused. But one must face the fact that this sort of language has been regularly used by Christians and that it is certainly not at all easy to see how a single person can have two natures. There is a recurrent tendency to say that this ultimate mystery is utterly incomprehensible and must be simply swallowed. God has revealed it somehow to the Church and we have therefore to acknowledge it, although we have no understanding of it. But a "mystery", in the proper theological sense, is something which is revealed for our understanding (what else could *revealing* it conceivably mean?) but which we can never understand *exhaustively* because it leads into the darkness of God. So we must try to understand what the language of the tradition is saying to us. At present I am insisting on what it cannot mean if we are to *think* about it at all. It cannot mean that God *turned into* a man. It cannot mean that *God suffered* on the cross in the literal sense of those words. Yet that is a conclusion which has been reached by theologians, Catholics as well as Protestants, on the basis of the views which I have been examining. Again it is true that such language is no new thing. It has been common enough in sermons down the ages. It is found in the Fathers, along with the conviction that God is immutable, so that Saint Cyril once said that the Son of God "suffered impassibly". But it has always been maintained by Christian metaphysicians, thinking at first-hand, that it cannot be taken literally and as it stands without further explanation.

An explanation must begin by considering what went on in the minds of Christ's first disciples. They were persuaded that he was an altogether *special* person. Jesus of Nazareth was a man, of course, but he was also in some mysterious way the Lord of men. He seemed to be related to God as no-one else was. He was the Son of the Father in a unique sense. Indeed there had to be some sense in which he and the Father were not only united with one another in a unique relationship but were actually *one*. This is how, as time went on, it came to be explicitly recognised and affirmed that there are relationships within the divine life itself. "God" does not mean just the Father of men and therefore the Father of Jesus Christ in some special way. "God" means both a Father and a Son, in the sense that the Father gives *everything* to the Son, that is, gives him *Infinity*. The life of God is a life of infinite love given and received and reciprocated—that is a first rough sketch of the doctrine of the Trinity into which the Christian experience unfolded. God is three "persons", Father, Son and Holy Spirit. But for the present it must suffice to consider the relationship between Father and Son. They are eternally related to one another in such a way that it is the life of God himself of which we speak when we say that the Father gives and the Son receives. They are *always* together. If we think of one without the other we are not thinking of *God*. The Father is the infinite source and the Son the infinite spring which arises from the source (so we have to picture it), but this source and this spring *are* the one infinite God. They differ from one another only in this that the Father is God as giver and the Son is God as received. We can speak of a life of love only as a life of persons. So the Son is a divine "person". It is this divine person which Christians have recognised in Jesus of Nazareth.

What, then, did they mean when they said that "God became man"? There was a temptation (into which many fell) to say that the divine person manifested himself in the form of a man, meaning by this that the manhood of Jesus was only an appearance, an illusion in fact. This was ruled out as untrue to the tradition, that is, to the continuing Christian experience. And there was a temptation (into which many fell) to say that Jesus was indeed God's messenger but that he had no special status apart from this. But again the faith of Christians was opposed to so easy an answer. Jesus was a man, yet his activity was that of God himself. The divine person and the manhood of Jesus were somehow *united*. The formula was found that the divine person owned a human nature in such a way that this nature belonged to him, not to a human person. It became a touchstone of truth in this matter to say that Jesus Christ is one person, a divine person with a human nature, and that there is in him no human personality. That did not mean that he had no human *character,* but that his human nature was so possessed by God's Word, the eternal Son, that the acts of Jesus were the acts of the Word. That does not remove the difficulty, but it puts it into its proper context. It presents us with the conclusion enunciated by Saint Thomas in a famous phrase that the manhood of Jesus is "the conjoined instrument of the divinity", *instrumentum conjunctum divinitatis.* Thus the difficulty is to see what meaning can be given to the assertion that there is a human nature which is owned by a divine person. Before tackling it, we have to remember that, if it is meaningless to say that God lowers himself in the Incarnation, the only alternative account of it must be that in it he raises human nature. It looks as though we shall have to say that a human nature is taken up and indeed taken over somehow by the divine person. This is in fact what is meant by the expression "hypostatic union".

We can make sense of it, I believe, if we suppose that the divine person so acts in the human nature that nothing of the action is lost or distorted, and this because the "instrument" is a perfect one. This proposal will at once encounter opposition because it seems to make Christ's humanity "unreal". To reduce him to an "instrument" which is being simply pushed around is to deprive him of all claim to be a man. In reply to this I would say in the first place that it would be a mistake to consider his manhood as just like ours. It is shown to us as *really* manhood but as being at the same time peculiar, unique, in virtue of the "hypostatic union"—manhood, thus united to a divine person, must have something different about it; to have a special status without having any special intrinsic characteristic would be to have an empty title. What I am proposing is that Christ was sinless, and not only in the sense that in fact he never sinned but in the sense that he was incapable of sin. A created human person must make the *choice* of God; this is the root of his moral responsibility; it is what *makes* him a human person. Christ was not a human *person*; he was not at risk as we are; he was not faced with the great divide which separates human persons from God and which can be crossed only on condition of their own willingness to be brought over it. This is not to say that his human nature had no pilgrimage to make. He had a human life to lead, and until it was lived out to the end it could not achieve its consummation, for he took our human condition upon him in every respect except that he was not capable of sin. That is what the Epistle to the Hebrews says—"like ourselves in every way, except for sin". He did not enjoy the *bliss* of God in his human nature until he had passed, like all of us, through death, but his human will was always indefectibly united with the divine will.

There are still many objections to be faced. How can there be a human will which is not morally free? I answer that "freedom to sin" is only a kind of freedom, proper to created human persons. There is another kind of freedom which consists in the full unhampered development of one's powers, the freedom to be completely oneself, which is possible for us only in the final union with God. Then our human wills are no less human; rather they have achieved their definitive exercise—they are utterly yet inexhaustibly satisfied, and there is now no question of turning aside from the Good itself in the interest of some temporary advantage. Christ's human will was free in this way. "It is my meat", we read, "to do the will of him who sent me." And, as we read these words and others which have the same ring, we recognise Christ as someone who was always "completely himself". It is the same to say that what we find in him is *sanctity*. But then, if he is so different from us, how can he be our example? It depends on what we mean by "example". It cannot mean that we are to act as he did in the sense of exercising his powers. What we have to do is to allow his power to be communicated to us so far as we, created human persons, can receive it. His is a human sanctity, and it is indeed a model for us to imitate. But it is his love for the Father (and therefore also for all men) into which we must be first drawn up; if we accept the power which he is offering us, then we shall live lives like his. But surely he did share our moral weakness? What about the temptations in the desert and the agony in the garden? The story of the temptations, I would say, is a story not of human weakness but precisely of the absence of it. And the agony in the garden shows us Christ's human revulsion as he contemplates the death which lies ahead of him. To say that it must have been possible for him to sin but that of course he never did so is to invite the questions : "what do you mean by 'of course'?" and *"can* you envisage a state of affairs in which Christ *sinned*?".

We have not yet done with objections. It may still be felt that on this account Christ is not truly *a man*. If to be a man means to be **a** human *person,* then it is indeed strictly incorrect to say that he is a man. But to refer, in the language of Christian theology, to his "human nature" is not to speak of an abstraction : Christ had and has a human mind and heart and he endured human sufferings. There has been so strong a reaction in our time against a swallowing up of the humanity by the divine person that theologians sometimes seem to suppose that their only duty is to guard against it (forgetting, as we have seen, that if the humanity degrades, cancels, the divinity there is nothing left to theologise about). It is true that there have been excessive claims about the effects of the hypostatic union. Until recently it was generally considered unorthodox not to allow that Christ's human mind enjoyed the definitive beatific vision during his life on earth. On the view which I am putting forward there is no ground for denying that his human knowledge developed in a human way, and that the meaning of his mission was gradually disclosed to him.

Two special difficulties remain. The acts of Jesus, according to this view, are the acts of the divine person, as the tradition maintains, because they are owned by the Word—he may be called responsible for them because there is in the human nature no moral responsibility proper to itself (no "personality"). These acts, however, are gifts to the human nature, so that they are *human* acts although proceeding from the divine source. But, unlike God's gifts to us, they are *unrefusable*. There is a human nature which is not "at risk" in the sense which I have been giving to that expression. Why, then, should *we* be "at risk"? Because, I can only say, it is good that there should be *persons*. And that there should be only *one* human nature "assumed" into the Word is hardly a difficulty. But if the acts of Jesus are to be called the acts of God, what are we to say of his sufferings? Simply, I suppose, that they are what men cause in him. What he does is his Father's will. This means that he will live a human life, taking what comes to him. God's power is given to him not to save himself from the consequences of his mission but to save others from their sins if they will let him. The rulers of his time did not accept his message; so they crucified him. *Their* acts caused his suffering. It was the suffering of a human nature possessed by the Word to whom its *acts* belong. But the divine person cannot suffer. The meaning of the Incarnation remains inexhaustible. I have tried only to show that it is possible to think about it without falsifying the Christian experience and without falling foul of the deliverances of that human experience which Christians and non-Christians share.

The Christian experience declares that God is Father, Son and Holy Spirit. I have already alluded to the regular answer given to the objection that to introduce distinctions into God must be to limit him, but at this point the answer must be developed. It is one and the same God who as Father gives and as Son receives. The Father is who he is in giving, and the Son is who he is in receiving, but what each gives or receives is the same. We cannot say that Fatherhood is limited by Sonship or Sonship by Fatherhood, for they are just *different* relationships; nor can you take one without the other because they are meaningful only in terms of one another. The three "persons" are not members of a class like human persons. They are in completely different relationships; yet they constitute the one Godhead. Thus there are not three centres of activity (of consciousness and so forth) in God. There is only one life, one love, in God, but it functions in a threefold way, moves, as it were, in three directions. And, to repeat, "three" does not mean this, that, and the other *instance* of something, as it does in the sphere of the finite. We can only say that it means "Father, Son and Holy Spirit". The Son "proceeds" eternally from the Father. And when we consider the "procession" of the Spirit we face no difficulties, so far as the infinity of God is concerned, which had not to be faced before. The oneness of God is compatible with all these relationships. "Person", then, is a word with a very special technical meaning in reference to the Trinity, and theologians of our time have pointed out that it has become in fact a misleading one.

Before saying anything more positively about the meaning of belief in the Holy Spirit, it seems necessary to remark that the doctrine of the Trinity is sometimes discussed by theologians today, Catholic as well as Protestant, in a way which appears to run counter to the tradition, the continuing Christian experience. We have already seen that this sort of thing is happening in connection with the Incarnation. In the present case the doctrine is apparently evacuated by the assertions that God is the Word only because he is revealed historically in Christ and that he is the Spirit only because as the result of Christ's victory he now dwells in the hearts of men. I say that the doctrine is *apparently* evacuated because, although this is the impression which I cannot help receiving, it may not be in fact intended. What we certainly find is the denial of the Word's "pre-existence", which one can take to mean, on the face of it, only that there is no eternal Word, from which it would follow that there is no eternal Spirit. In that case the belief of Christians would have been mistaken down the ages in the most fundamental way.

The trouble has arisen partly from a failure to make sense of the formula "two natures and one person" and partly from the fact that the indwelling of God in the human soul is regularly referred to in terms of the Holy Spirit, from which it is concluded that talk of the Holy Spirit can mean nothing else than the fact of this indwelling—God *as* indwelling *is* the Holy Spirit. But Christians believe in the Holy Spirit not just because they are aware of God's presence but because God reveals to them in some measure the secrets of his own divine life. This is not to say that the faithful must claim an explicit awareness of the Trinity as such, although it would be easy to show that Christian mysticism in its fully developed form does make such a claim. But Christian faith must be implicitly trinitarian; that is, it must involve, however inarticulately, an awareness of God as living a life of infinite love, as containing within himself in an infinite form the *value* of society, the value (for which we have so high a regard) of relations between persons. Here we have to remember that the "persons" of the

Trinity are not distinct from one another as human persons are distinct; although completely different as "persons", they are *perfectly* united, and this would seem to be our ideal of love. The life of God, once more, does not contain three centres of operation but is a single threefold operation, changeless and eternal. It is the Christian experience that this operation, which, as directed upon ourselves, we greet as pure generosity, is, independently of us, an interchange of pure generosity. The Father's gift to the Son is returned to him again, and this movement of return *is* the Holy Spirit. That seems to be the short formula which emerges from authentic Christian theology. It is bound up with another short formula : we are to be brought *in* the Spirit, *through* the Son, to the Father, caught up in this movement of return. To that I shall return. But it must be emphasised here that it is not the Holy Spirit alone who dwells in us, for he can never be alone, but God who is Father, Son and Holy Spirit.

When I say that this must be implicit in Christian faith, I mean that faith comes to recognise itself as expressed in this way. But it did not do so originally and does not do so now as a result of a sudden vision of the Trinity or of a passive waiting for "the spark from heaven to fall". What I am talking about is the life of the Church, which is indeed made up of the lives of its members deriving from their Head, but which is nevertheless a life which is shared, and the members learn through one another. That is, it is regularly through our relations with one another that God makes himself known to us in the revelation of himself in Christ. As with knowledge of the Word, so with knowledge of the Spirit (the latter flowing from the former), that part of the tradition which is the New Testament has its indispensable part to play. It claims to record Christ's teaching about the Holy Spirit. It was through meditation on this as well as on the whole business of being a Christian that the first trinitarian formulas came into existence. Belief in the Father, the Son and the Holy Spirit soon became the first Creed, and all Creeds, it seems, are the unpacking of it.

The Christian mystery is a single one, but it has many facets and can be summed up in various ways. It is summed up, for example, by saying that it is "the sending of the Spirit", which like all such formulas has many implications. It is a summing-up because it tells us that union with God is what this is all about, but it has to be understood that the Spirit is sent through the incarnate Son, and this presupposes the whole work of that Son. So we cannot understand much about "the sending of the Spirit" until we know something about that work. Should we not, then, have spoken about it before speaking of the Spirit at all? But how can one begin to speak of the Son without going on at once to speak of the Spirit? How could one say anything about one of the "persons" without saying something about the others? There is in fact a general difficulty about a chapter of this kind; one cannot speak of everything at once but nothing makes very much sense until you get to the end, although I hope that what I have so far said makes some sense. I have tackled the difficulty in the way which seemed to have relatively few disadvantages.

So now I turn to the topic of redemption. And first, what are we supposed to be redeemed *from*? This question has been answered already up to a point by what was said about original sin in the previous chapter. There it was suggested that Christ restores to us a certain *intimacy* with God which the human race once had and subsequently lost, and that he gives us the power to overcome hereditary disorders. But I have also referred to the new life which Christ offers us as the one and only means, according to Christians, whereby we may reach God in a final union with him. And, fundamentally, this is what "redemption" means. Somehow all men, even those who lived before Christ's coming (although the new life won by Christ's victory was not available for them in their lifetime) must gain this life and will gain it if they are willing to do so. But this is not all that redemption means. This explains why Christ *save*s us—because our hope is in him alone. It is *his* grace which we reject, if we reject God. But redemption means literally "*buying* back". In some sense Christ paid a price for us. How is that to be explained?

This question has to be looked at in its proper context. That is, we have to consider *why* it was that the Father summoned us to him *through* the Son and *in* the Holy Spirit. So far I have talked as though this had no need of explanation. That it should be "the divine event to which the whole creation moves" seemed intelligible enough. It fits in with our evolutionary view of things. But there is weighty authority for the view that there would have been no "sending" of the Son if there had been no sin to be redeemed. It was not God's original plan but his answer to a situation which might never have occurred (for it would be meaningless to say that *sin* was *inevitable*). So we must now face the famous question about "the motive of the Incarnation", for one's view of the redemption may be considerably affected by the answer to it.

According to Saint Thomas, there is no ground for the proposal that the Incarnation was God's original plan because the Scriptures tell us plainly that it was God's answer to sin and we have no right to go beyond that. Theologians have claimed that this does not involve any denial of the essential function of the Word in the economy of salvation if we accept the view of the Fathers that there was an original revelation of the Trinity and so also of the Word's mediating function. It has always been through the Word that men have come to the Father. When this original revelation was lost, it was restored by the *incarnate* Word. Otherwise the Word would not have been incarnate. But it cannot be said that the opposite view, put forward by Duns Scotus as against Saint Thomas, is not a legitimate theological opinion. And I hold to it, as at present advised, because I cannot think that the Incarnation is merely a means of restoring what was lost. It seems to me that there are positive values about the Christian dispensation which, in Saint Thomas's view, would depend on man's sin for their existence, and this I find unacceptable. While acknowledging the weight of authority on Saint Thomas's side, it seems to me that his answer is not part of the tradition itself. After all, no one is denying that Christ came to save us from our sins, which is what the tradition tells us. To add that he would have come whether or not there was sin in the world is to go beyond what the scriptures tell us (although many would say that Saint Paul implies it), but there is nothing to prevent us from raising questions with which the scriptures and the Fathers were not concerned. I shall not discuss all the difficulties which I find in the Thomist view. It must suffice to have indicated in general terms why one is not obliged to adopt it.

The Incarnation, then, I shall say, was in fact redemptive because in fact there were sins to be redeemed. Its "motive" was our union with God through the incarnate Word, and for this to be possible men must have the power to break through the barriers of sin. The grace of Christ must destroy evil in the hearts of men if they are to be raised to the new life. But these are not two distinct processes. Unless a man's will has been definitively perverted (which is never the case, we may suppose, before his death) it is possible for him to answer Christ's summons, and his turning to God is at the same time his turning away from evil. Christ redeems him *in* bringing him to the Father. But that does not answer our question about the literal meaning of redemption, its sense of "buying back". Is this to be discarded? Must we not say that Christ paid a price for us? Did he not suffer for us on the cross?

It is very widely supposed that Christ suffered *instead of* us. But this theory of vicarious suffering is no part of the Christian faith. It implies an idea of God which is not only anthropomorphic but morally revolting. Pious people who use its language are doubtless unconscious of its implications. But to say that God accepts Christ's sufferings in exchange for our sins can mean only that he requires them as a compensation for some loss which he himself is supposed to have suffered. And after what has been said in earlier chapters there is no need to argue that this is not only meaningless but, strictly speaking, blasphemous. Christ came to raise human life to its consummation by living that life completely—and so he died a human death. That was the price which he had to pay in order to fulfil his mission (and the manner of his death was due to the sins of his contemporaries). Once this sort of language became current, perfectly proper and natural language in the sense just indicated, there was the danger that it might be detached from its context. If Christ paid a price, then to whom did he pay it? But that question should never have been asked. It was thought that "the claims of justice" demanded that Christ should show his love for us by a death on the Cross or at least that it was "fitting" for him to do so. But "the claims of justice" can mean only the claims of God. To say that God is "offended" cannot mean that he ceases to be beneficent and needs to be persuaded into relenting. It can mean only that we have put ourselves out of reach of his beneficence. Christ did indeed show his love in the most wonderful way. But how can it be supposed that his suffering was required of him in the sense that this way of showing his love was the divine will? And if it was not *necessary* for him to suffer so as to meet "the claims of justice", why should the Father wish it to be so? How can the suffering of the innocent, of his own Son, be the condition for the pardon of sinners? We must surely conclude that Christ suffered not *instead of* us, but *on our behalf*.

It has to be admitted that the theory just criticised has been highly influential among Christians and is still to be found in theological textbooks even in the crude form in which I have presented it. It is frequently implied in sermons, and it has taken deep root in the popular mind. But clearly its days are numbered. This is a striking example of what can happen if Christians forget what

"God" *means*. If we lose touch with our own experience, we may talk the worst kind of nonsense. Talk about "merit", unfortunately, has been so often of this kind, implying that our relations with God are to be understood, literally, in juridical terms. But the suggestion that we can make claims on God is just as objectionable as the suggestion that he can benefit from us ("giving him glory" is sometimes supposed to mean just that). God's "justice" in the New Testament, we are assured, refers to his own faithfulness to his promises. So the reign of his justice is the reign in which we receive these promises. Our "merit" is our readiness to receive. As Saint Augustine puts it, when God rewards our merits, he crowns his own gifts.

So far the work of Christ has been referred to only in rather vague terms. I have said that he had his own pilgrimage to make, and the meaning of this must be brought out. He took our human nature just as it was "except for sin", and therefore he must work his own passage to the Father before he can join us to him in his consummate, "glorified", state. He would not have been one of us if he had not accepted the laws of human life, which meant the law of death. If there had been no sin in the world death would have been different, it seems. Christ accepted the conditions which sin had brought about. He would not have been our example otherwise. And if he had not taken on *our* human condition, the Fathers are always saying, he could not have raised it. It is the human race as it actually is which is to share his consummated life with the Father, and so he must be truly united with us. The manhood of Christ must win its saving power in the life of God before it can be communicated to us. The Passion is the passage to the Resurrection. Only after that can Christ send us the Spirit.

So Catholic theologians, fresh from a profounder study of the New Testament (the "biblical revival"), tell us that Christ was in a true sense "distant" from the Father during his earthly life. It was not until the flesh which he took from us died that he could enter into the final union. In this sense he too had to be *made holy* —which is what sacrifice, precisely, means. Sacrifice is for union. It is the "passover". At the moment of his death, which is also that of his victorious consummation, Christ's body becomes the principle of our redemption. As redeeming us, it is the Church, Head and members. But the members must be in action themselves. They must join themselves (allow themselves to be joined) to Christ's passover, to the act of perfect love which, because it is now consummated, remains eternally active. And that is the Eucharist, the Christian sacrifice.

Just as there used to be a concentration on the Cross, considered as redeeming us apart from the resurrection (which then followed by way of epilogue so as to prove Christ's divinity), so there has been in the recent past a concentration on the Eucharist as putting us in touch with the Crucifixion, considered as an isolated event. It is now recognised on all hands that it is the whole mystery of Christ which is celebrated therein. It is the risen Christ, the lamb who was slain, who offers himself to us as our food and drink. We do indeed "show forth his death until he comes" but that death was the fulfilment of his human life, and we celebrate it as such. The Eucharist is the thanksgiving for the gift of Christ and in celebrating it according to his own instructions on the evening before his Passion we have his guarantee that his grace is available to us in pre-eminent form. Unless Christians actually gather together to receive the power won for them by Christ, they cannot constitute a *Church*. Their common meal expresses their unity with one another; Christ has made it the vehicle of his ever-increasing transformation of them into "other Christs"—that is, he offers them this transformation, but it rests with them whether they will accept it in ever-increasing measure. This is the heart of Christian mysticism.

In the Eucharist, then, Christ's act of sacrifice, his definitive achievement, draws us more and more closely into union with him, with the life of God. His sacrifice is completed; ours is an entering into it. We are drawn up into his own love of the Father. In the Eucharist this love is present to us in a special way because he has so ordained it. That does not mean that Christ is not always present to us; it means that this is his appointed way of building up his Church. We might say that it is the proximate source of sanctity. The bread and wine become the whole Christ, his body and blood. Chemically they are unchanged, but their reality is Christ. (That is what transubstantiation means.) They were first our offerings, standing for our own human lives and indeed for all the world which Christ is to transform; they become the eternally accepted offering, Christ himself, and in receiving them again we receive his life.

When he instituted the Eucharist Christ gave us a form of worship perfectly adapted to our needs. The sacraments do not restrict God's generosity (he is not *tied* to the sacraments); rather they exercise it in the way which is most profitable for us. We must have a focus for our religion—otherwise, in practice, it evaporates. We need to express ourselves to God in terms of the visible world to which we belong. God has expressed himself to us in Christ's human nature. The life of the risen Christ is expressed, when it is communicated to us, in terms of our basic human sustenance.

I have confined myself here to those elements of eucharistic doctrine which I venture to call the essential ones. There have been many theories about the eucharistic sacrifice which are based on that same legalistic approach which has obscured the doctrine of the redemption, and so they discuss God's dealings with us in the same anthropomorphic way. They may even suggest that the effects of the eucharist are automatic or that its "fruits" are arbitrarily limited by God. And here again such notions have sunk deep into the popular mind. Some readers might feel that what I have said about the Eucharist simply leaves out a great deal which they supposed to be bound up with it. There was of course a great deal more to be said. But a great deal which has been said by theologians of the past has been deliberately passed over as inessential.

As always with the central Christian doctrines, it has to be pointed out that at the present time the theological pendulum swings wildly here : there is a tendency to "desacralise" the Eucharist, a reaction against a widespread failure in the past to recognise that its context is a community meal. Christians do come together for a meal. But it is a meal which is also a sacrifice, that is, a means of union with God. They bring their everyday lives to it but in order to transform them. So it is most strange that a renewed realisation of the Eucharist's relevance to our lives should lead to the conclusion that it should be celebrated in a casual manner, in slipshod language, without beauty or dignity and even without any kind of awe. The "liturgical revival", which was so urgently needed, will have proved a failure if it does not help Christians to *pray*. A reaction against individualistic piety can lead people to behave as though prayer meant nothing but "getting together". It means getting to God, and each of us is related directly to him.

Now that the topic of union with God has been given its context from the Christian point of view we can consider more closely what is meant by it and how it is promoted; certain difficulties in well-known accounts of it will have to be discussed; we can then consider how various phenomena commonly referred to as "mystical" may be interpreted by a Christian thinker.

A good deal of obscurity has been caused, it seems to me, by a failure to recognise that we can make sense of a union with God only as a loving awareness, an awareness which is made what it is by love. That fundamental human experience, discussed in its initial form in earlier chapters, is, so far as I can see, the only possible basis for an understanding of mysticism. If we speak of "grace" as a capacity or power which God gives us, it must be a capacity or power for conscious union with him—we can speak of it intelligibly only in that way. If we try to talk about it in any other terms, we shall be saying either that God gives us something other than himself, some mysterious gift which makes us "pleasing" to him, considered perhaps as some impossible half-way house between finite and infinite, or we shall find ourselves talking as though we became actually identical with him. To say that God gives himself to us in knowledge and love is understandable—indeed it is to say what understanding itself really is. But it is surely meaningless to talk about a union with God which somehow transcends the sphere of loving knowledge. We have nothing to talk about except our own experience and what comes into it. If we are to talk of union with God we must be talking of his presence within our own experience.

To particularise further, if we are to talk of "created grace", we must make clear that we are not proposing an intermediary between God and the human spirit, for this may seem either to keep us out of touch with him or perhaps to be the instrument of a *confusion* with him; by using this language we can be referring only to ourselves as *united* with him. If we speak of "uncreated grace", we can be referring (in a rather awkward way) only to God as united with ourselves. If we speak of "participating" in God or of "deification" (both accepted expressions in Christian theology), we must make clear that we are not suggesting a literal sharing in God's Infinity. Again, the "indwelling" of the Trinity in the human soul is sometimes discussed as though it were a special, distinct, topic. But all these expressions must refer to the same situation. They have—or at various times have had—their uses in emphasising one or another of its aspects. But when modern theologians think it necessary to speak of a "quasi-formal union", I cannot help wondering whether they have not, for the moment, lost touch with it. What is presumably intended is a union without confusion—but that is just what knowledge always is. To escape from this mystifying jargon we have only to remember what in fact we are : metaphysical animals.

This sort of mystification, it may be remarked in passing, is what tends to happen when theology loses itself among abstractions. Mystical theology, properly understood, is the very opposite of mystification. It is about the fullness of real life and that freedom from illusions which is only possible when we are in touch with the source of life. Dogmatic theology, properly understood, articulates mystical theology, which has as its content the experience of faith in developed, matured form; and, since God is strictly ineffable, these articulations can only "point to" the mystery of God in Christ which is the heart of Christian experience. Theological concepts are properly intelligible only in the light of faith. So theology loses its way when it forgets either that it is *God* with whom it is concerned or that it is *our* experience in which we find him. All genuine theology must have a contemplative character.

Union with God is not in itself something extraordinary. It is the ordinary goal which the Christian sets before him, the purpose for which the Christian life is ordered (but so far from being incompatible with the effective love of one's neighbour, it is impossible without it). If it is a goal which is seldom achieved in practice, that is because it is supposed to be attainable only by very special people or because it seems so difficult. In principle it is available for everybody. If it is accepted that there is a mystical element in faith, then all the faithful enjoy this union at least in an embryonic form—we shall be concerned with it here only in what may be called its normal adult form, the form which is *meant* for all of us. It has, of course, also its extraordinary forms, and it is these, unfortunately, which usually come to mind when "mysticism" is mentioned. And something must be said about them at once so that they may not stand in our way. They are characterised chiefly by a state of peculiar passivity in which no distinction is *felt* between the soul and God, and they are sometimes accompanied by extraordinary physical conditions (levitation, for example), visions and locutions. The competent authorities agree that such manifestations have nothing to do with the substance of mystical prayer and that they normally disappear before its highest stage has been reached (it would seem that some of them are due to the strain imposed upon the physical organism in extraordinary conditions). One need have no difficulty in granting that these higher stages of mystical prayer are not intended for everyone. God gives to all of us our individual capacities, and when they are perfectly fulfilled we shall ask for no more (although even after the fulfilment which we find in death God is inexhaustible for all of us—that is to say, our love for him will inexhaustibly increase). He does grant all of us, however, *union* with him (if we are willing to have it) in this life as well as in the next, and all union with him has the same basic characteristics. The life of faith develops as one same life until we are ready for the final, beatific vision. To describe only its extraordinary developments as "mystical' (as has been done by many influential writers) is, in practice, to deny that it has these basic characteristics —that, I mean, is the impression which in fact is given by this use of language. We are all called to a direct conscious union with God, to a life for which the only single descriptive epithet is "mystical".

But it is important to realise what is meant and (especially) what is *not* meant by "conscious union". What is meant is that obscure awareness of God in Christ which alone can account (so I have maintained) for the certainty which faith can give—but in a form which, instead of being occasional (aroused only perhaps by a deliberate advertence to the truths of faith and the divine authority which shines through them), is now pervasive, not merely something at the back of the mind, nor yet always in the forefront of the mind, but, as it were, just below the surface, ready to emerge when it has the chance. It may at first lose nothing of its obscurity, but it is now on its way to becoming a habitual state. A man who has faith always knows that he has it—that is, he is aware that he has a certain attitude of mind in regard to Christianity even when he is not adverting to it. But as faith matures, he tends to advert to it more and more. He has always recognised it as supremely important in itself; now it begins to play that part in his actual experience to which it is entitled. It is a *loving* awareness, and this means, first, that any alienation from God is appreciated as the worst possible thing that can happen. It follows that our relations with other people become a matter of grave concern—in important ways they depend on us, as we do on them, and our duties to them as God's children become very plain (often we do not know how to act for the best, but it becomes very clear that what we *can* do we *ought* to do); in the language of religion, what is all-important is God's will.

But because this is a loving *awareness,* we are not just doing things to please a distant God. We do not "see him in others" just because we know that they are his children. He speaks to us himself in our contacts with them. Our obedience, our attention to him, and to them, strengthens our contact with him as well as with them. And this is the royal road to the habitual consciousness that we and they are made for him (and only so for one another)—and that nothing else matters.

So there is nothing fantastic about this programme. But it is necessary to insist that it is not always or even often a state of exaltation. And it is never one of joy in the commonplace sense of that word. Joy in that sense, we shall have to conclude (sorrowfully, and perhaps with a certain nostalgia for it), is in fact a sort of escapism, for what it stands for is only a relief from boredom or from some kind of insecurity, a euphoria which is not an end in itself but is treated as if it were such. Is that a cynical conclusion? Certainly it is true that there are pure joys which find some place, so at least we may hope, in everyone's life, the joys which spring from appreciating good people and beautiful things simply for what they are (and I have contended that the discovery of God can be made in precisely that way). But we have to admit, I think, that this is not, by and large, what "joy" means to the bulk of our contemporaries. If there is "joy" in conscious union with God it is not what they commonly mean by it. There can indeed be joy in this union—a pure joy like those just mentioned, but an enriched and expanded one. Indeed, it is regularly found in the beginning of faith, the first *act* of faith, for this, despite its normal obscurity, is a conscious contact. But that does not usually last very long for reasons which will be later considered. What does persist is a sort of satisfaction which is perhaps best described as an underlying expectant peace. It is sometimes described as the sense of having come home, but it seems better to say that it is a sense of having a home prepared for one on the other side of death (in the language which some people seem to prefer, it is "the eschatological dimension"). The loving awareness, then, is registered as any experience must be : it does not lack an affective tone, but this may be largely overlaid for indefinite periods by the affective tones which result from other concurrent experiences.

More light may be shed on all this if we now turn to the traditional account of the stages through which prayer passes, so far as it affects what I have referred to as the normal adult form of it.

This account as found in the manuals may well seem overcomplicated, but taken in its broad outline it does present a pattern of Christian experience for which there is abundant evidence. First, however, we need to add to it the distinction between the experience of the "cradle" Christian of the manuals and that of the adult convert to Christianity. The former thinks of God at first in an anthropomorphic way, and his prayer will be the prayer of petition. He will be instructed in Christianity as a system of thought and a way of life, and for some time at least his approach to it is likely to be a rationalistic and moralistic one, accompanied perhaps by some religiosity (which I take to be what "sensible devotion" means when that expression is used in a somewhat derogatory sense). If he is lucky, he will be encouraged at an early age to regard prayer as an affair of personal contact with God, but it is on the whole improbable that he will be given any acceptable explanation of it; its connection with the rest of his experience is likely to remain obscure at least until he is able and willing to read and to think about it. In any case the chances are that his interest in religion will be for some time meditative rather than contemplative. But unless he allows himself to stick in a rut, he must realise somehow what faith is and accept its implications, that it requires of us a "waiting upon" God, an attention to his direct action upon ourselves, a submission of our whole being to this action, an adoration which becomes increasingly silent. The traditional account, before speaking about that, warns us that we must be suitably prepared for it. We must feel the need to enter into the Christian mystery instead of looking at it, as it were, from the outside; this must have become our real concern or we may waste our time in day-dreaming instead of praying. To this I shall return.

The point at the moment is that the adult convert of today is quite likely to have approached this stage already before he is finally convinced. He may well have passed through the meditative stage, which will consist for him in making sense of Christianity and realising his own need for God and so for the sacraments (the Eucharist being the living centre from which union with God derives); otherwise he is not likely to be ready for the life of faith. But, when he does enter upon it, he will understand a good deal of what it means. And the Christian of tomorrow, everything seems to suggest, will usually be, in effect, a convert. That is to say, it is becoming in practice less and less normal even for people brought up in a Christian atmosphere to embrace Christianity by a deliberate personal act without having first passed through a period in which everything goes into the melting-pot. And Christian atmospheres are going to be a good deal less common in the immediate future than they have been in our society. The sociological backing which they once enjoyed is rapidly disappearing. It is not going to be possible to take Christianity for granted, and the Church of Christ will undergo a necessary refining process. To become or to remain a Christian is going to make greater demands on people than it did in the recent past. Nominal or conventional Christians, it seems, will be in shorter and shorter supply in the foreseeable future. And to meet the demands that will be made personal, persevering prayer will be absolutely necessary. The development of prayer is therefore a topic which is not only of the greatest importance in itself but one which has a peculiar relevance to the present situation. There are plenty of signs that the mentality of modern man, despite its many maladies or rather perhaps in consequence of them, is more and more experiencing the need for what one can only call "mysticism". And many who are out of touch with Christianity but have received baptism "by desire" may be in fact engaged in contemplative prayer (here it must be observed that the word "contemplative" is very often used in the same restricted sense as "mystical" to refer to *extraordinary* states of prayer).

So what the traditional account has to tell us about the difficulties which are met with in this way of prayer is of the highest practical importance. I have said something already about an absence of joy (in the everyday sense) when in fact there is union with God. As prayer develops, our guides all declare, there are times when prayer becomes not merely boring but extremely painful. I am not proposing to examine the distinction which they draw between a "night of the senses" and a "night of the spirit" (although I believe it to be a well-founded one) because the problems which they set are in principle the same. What is important is to realise that the affective tone of a man's experience may be for long periods a distressing one but that this is no reason for discouragement. It is something which Christians have regularly lived through and which they have learned to value. But their explanations of it, I must confess, are not always satisfying. To say, for example, that God is testing our love for him seems to raise difficult questions about his providence. What does seem to have truth in it is that attending to God means a development of the whole personality—it is growing all the time and until it has reached a definite maturity growing pains are inevitable. Fresh demands are made upon us at every stage and we are always wanting a rest. What is called conversion is only the first stage, and that may have been difficult enough. If our generosity does not correspond with God's in later stages, then there is a sort of blackout. Or (as it is often said) the increasing brightness of the divine light begins to dazzle our eyes—for the time being we are in a state of unpleasant bewilderment; there may be some clue in that also. But however we are to account for "the feeling of God's absence" it is not to be interpreted to mean that he is really absent— still less that he has never been present at all. The great mistake here is to suppose that prayer as union with God is to be equated with pleasurable feelings.

What it really is the spiritual tradition declares to us with complete unanimity : *wanting* God. And one cannot want anything without having some knowledge of what it is that one wants. It is an awareness of God which sets off this wanting, but it is an awareness which is very far from satisfying. It seems sometimes to be an awareness just sufficiently definite to cause an intensely painful desire for an unhampered form of it, a desire which predominates over all other elements of experience and is thus registered in a predominant emotional tone. This "feeling of God's absence" is often far *too* unpleasant to be explained away in naturalistic terms. It might be supposed that it is simply an intense disappointment in a matter which has aroused the keenest expectations. But that account of it does not fit the facts. Those who have coped with it tell us that it was not really a condition of despair, although at the time they might have used this language about it. For, as they now realise, they could not get away from the *thought* of God. And this apparently fruitless obsession, as also they now realise, did them in fact a great deal of good, for their *interest* in God was growing all the time. This "feeling of God's absence" is something quite different from that feeling of alienation (or lack of identity) from which so many of our contemporaries are suffering. That, too, may result from some awareness of God, a first faint glimmer—but he has not yet been *accepted*. The people of whom I am speaking have accepted him. When the workings of faith were made intelligible to them, they realised that they had been always in the right way.

This spiritual tradition, then, can be immensely valuable for our time. Not only can it give the greatest encouragement to those who are tempted to give up the search for God, to stifle their "suspicion" of him, but it can come to the rescue of so many, Christian and non-Christian, who have already, unwittingly, entered this way of prayer. The earnestness with which the Christian mystics insist that it must not be abandoned cannot fail to be deeply impressive. They warn us with one voice that unless we go forward we shall go downward on a slope which is extremely slippery. And they provide us with evidence of the most convincing kind that those who persevere do in fact emerge from the periods of painful bewilderment. The loving awareness of God does return to the surface. One cannot, of course, lay down absolute rules about this process. There are cases in which what I have called an "expectant peace" is all that ever returns to the surface, and it must suffice to suggest one reason for this: it may be accompanied by such a profound sympathy for the distresses of mankind that a livelier joy is inhibited —but here we have to face the apparent paradox that in the great saints the intensest suffering and the intensest joy are frequently found together. The general pattern, however, is clear. There is an emergence from the "night", and from time to time "expectant peace" breaks into an indescribable fulfilment.

Those who consider that the language of "contemplation" (and even of "union") should be employed in referring only to the highest states of prayer will feel that what has been so far said is very dangerous—it may encourage people to suppose that they are in the "mystic way" when in fact they are nowhere near it. Possibly it might, if certain further warnings were not issued. In the first place it would clearly be a mistake to suppose that the development of an increasingly silent prayer carries with it the abandonment of any *thinking* about religion. The formal meditations of previous centuries are probably unsuited to our present psychological make-up. But what is certainly needed is such *study* of Christianity as can be managed, especially a close acquaintance with the New Testament, the sort of theology which is not just arid scholarship but provides a most valuable stimulus to prayer. Those who consider themselves "average educated men" should consider themselves capable of this. It is a sign of returning health in Christianity when Christians cease to regard theology as a preserve of specialists in which they cannot be expected to take an interest. Moreover the actual practice of prayer, even when one has some grasp of the Christian mystery, will involve some kind of meditation.

For it is not simply a matter of emptying our minds and fixing them on God. That may be possible, later, but it is dangerous, I would say, to suppose that one can start like that at once. What we probably need to do, it seems to me, is not to make an immediate frontal attack on the thoughts and desires which we found ourselves with, but to examine our own attitude towards them. In fact there will have to be some meditation to deal with the existing situation. If we find ourselves, for example, in some disordered state of mind, we shall need to discover whether something is wrong with us which we can at least *want* to put right. Unless we can take up the right attitude to it, we cannot be really wanting God. Sometimes a disturbed condition will result from causes outside our control (in that case the result of the whole exercise may be, so far as we can perceive, only a lessening of the disturbance). But, in any case, we have to face up to the initial distractions and see them for what they are. We are trying to be honest with ourselves, and that is prayer already.

Even when things have seemed to settle down there will be sub- sequent distractions. So long as we go on wanting God, they do not matter. Commonsense dictates that to attack these casual intruders will only have the effect of delaying their departure. They have to be, as far as possible, simply ignored. Others take their place, and this may go on all the time. Nevertheless, if we have done what we could (more or less and rather less than more, we shall probably feel), we are dimly aware that the time has not been wasted. It may have been boring on the whole (but not distressingly so, if we are not yet in a "night", only just starting), but we shall find that the "expectant peace" will be there at times when we were not looking for it. We should probably not have started looking for it at all unless it had been given to us previously—out of the blue, as it were. Indeed probably we had been already "surprised by joy". It is all God's gift, and when we are capable of it he offers it to us. Normally this joy will return from time to time. But it is not the feeling of it which is the heart of the matter, but the union of spirit, of mind and will. It was necessary to say that again in the present context, leading up to another, pretty obvious, warning about this earliest stage of contemplative prayer : it is imperative to realise that it is a matter of education, of training, and that we must there- fore be businesslike about it. Unless time is regularly set aside for it —perhaps only a few minutes each day, to become more in the future—there is unlikely to be the proper progress. Here again one cannot lay down absolute rules except for this : that we must aim, by whatever means are possible and suited for us, at the inner silence in which union with God is promoted.

There are apparently people for whom outer silence is not a prerequisite, but I suppose them to be extremely rare. The growing absence of outer silence has become a matter of grave concern to many who are not thinking in terms of "spirituality" but who do have a sense of human values. So it is strange that religious people should not take more interest in the topic. In particular I have in mind the reform of the Catholic liturgy. It is indeed a reform in so far as it recognises that the liturgy is performed by the church, not just by the clergy, and that it is intended to be intelligible. But it has had the deplorable side-effect of abolishing for so many their only normal occasion for inner silence and putting nothing comparable in its place. Once upon a time the priest muttered away in Latin and then (during the eucharistic prayer) became completely inaudible, while the people got on with their devotions as they thought fit. As a way of celebrating the Eucharist it was absurd. It did, however, produce saints. Nowadays there is almost always some sort of loud noise going on except for a pause after the Communion which is (so far as I know) very seldom more than a token one. And there is also to be reckoned with the virtual disappearance (again so far as I know) of the old "thanksgiving after Communion", praying on one's own when the liturgy was over, for which ten minutes was once considered the decent minimum. (There is nothing original, I am happy to say, about these remarks.)

It is necessary now to say something more about writers on "mystical theology", for anyone who might turn from reading this book to reading one of theirs would probably conclude that their principles of thought are in fact rather different from those adopted here. Someone once said of Saint Augustine that he had not the philosophy of his theology. It may seem very presumptuous to apply this remark to mystical writers in general, but I shall suggest that there are good reasons for doing so in important instances without thereby detracting from their own special authority or the special significance of their testimony. These writers, like all authentic theologians, are not interested in speculation for its own sake or as an academic exercise; and they are concerned with the practice of religion more directly than theologians whose first business is to expound it. As a natural result, they are not much interested in philosophical questions and sometimes take for granted philosophical ideas which happen to be in fashion at the time. The most famous of them, Saint John of the Cross, was indeed trained in scholasticism and became a high-powered exponent of it, but he felt no need to regard its psychology with a critical eye—it seemed to cause nobody any particular difficulty and it would be a waste of time to dwell on it (when pretty well everyone you met was a theist, a good many philosophical questions simply did not arise in any serious way). So he took over quite happily a doctrine of will in sharp distinction from intellect which we found operative in certain theories about faith less popular than they were but still highly influential. What is true of faith will be true, naturally, of contemplative prayer. What unites us with God is a will or desire which does so without assistance from the mind (we are supposed to know already by reason *that he exists,* of course, but that is something different). In fact the will itself enlightens the mind. Such is the dark doctrine which the modern reader may find emerging from the writings of the mystics.

What went wrong, so it appears to me, may be put like this. A distinction between *intellect* (or mind) and discursive reason, well established in the High Middle Ages, was gradually lost sight of, mind becoming reduced in effect to reason, so that the intuitive powers, once attributed to the intellect, were attributed to something else—the will. The Romantics, at the end of eighteenth century, could appeal only to the "imagination" or to "feeling" for what was so obviously lacking. "Reason", "intellect", and "mind" were all tarred with the same brush. On the one side, there were just abstractions; on the other, just emotions. You could choose, apparently, only between these alternatives—not that people put it in that crude way, but that was what it amounted to, for so many of them. In the later Middle Ages there were only the first hints of this complete breakdown. By the fourteenth century, although the life of the spirit was still recognised and indeed was being taken with an increasing seriousness, rationalising tendencies had made people chary of allowing any direct contact of the *mind* with God. The mystics knew that contact with him is nevertheless made, and they talked about it in the only sort of language which seemed available. It had to be made clear at all costs that contemplative prayer was not a matter of concepts, of working things out or of knowing *that* something was true but one of a vital contact with truth itself. As a result mysticism tended to go hand in hand with an anti-intellectualism which a modern reader may find most disconcerting. It has indeed nothing directly to do with being learned or clever. But it is, in the once familiar phrase, the "science of the saints". It is about the indescribable—but to suggest that it is unintelligible is to suggest the very opposite of the truth.

The need to warn people not to rely on their *feelings* complicated matters still further as time went on. I have tried to explain what I take to be the real rationale of such warnings. But spiritual writers have been often led to say that prayer is itself not a matter of "experience" at all. That is to say, it may or may not be accompanied by "experience": in itself (the reader may be forced to conclude) it is a wholly unconscious state of affairs. And in that case it seems unlikely that anyone will go on reading about it. Fortunately, however, these writers, with apparent inconsistency, regularly go on to speak of spiritual joy in a way which makes clear that it is not just "sensible devotion"; often they refer to it as some faint anticipation of the beatific vision. Obviously, then, the very highest value must be ascribed to it, and when they tell us that we must never set store by such experiences they can only mean that we must be prepared to do without them, and perhaps nearly always. These must be considered experiences of God, and we cannot suppose that they are not meant for us.

When we are told that there are extraordinary states of prayer (which, as we have seen, are considered by some the only "mystical" ones) we may indeed suppose that they are not meant for us. But what is said about them could be another disconcerting discovery. When, for example, we read that self-consciousness may not only seem to disappear but actually does so, we may well feel that this is meaningless. What has to be remembered is that these writers are not usually exact thinkers; it is quite possible for their language to become imprecise or exaggerated. They may also seem to spend a good deal of time on topics which hardly require it. For example, they are often much exercised by problems about Christian perfection. If it consists in charity, then is this not possible without any "mystical" development at all even in the broad sense in which I have used that word? And even if they answer correctly that it is not, they may do so with some hesitation, failing perhaps to realise that charity is inseparable from a faith which has itself a mystical character. The purest prayer must be the purest act of charity. The development of prayer is not only the fulfilment which God intends for us as individuals (although particular circumstances may make it impossible) but the building up of his Church, for we are not just individuals. We may be told that we must not expect it, for this is God's gift; but that is surely the reason why we should hope for it and prepare ourselves for it. In that case, if circumstances should prevent it, we shall be ready for its full development when we come to die. In this context we *could* certainly say that a union of *will* is what matters. In one sense, Christian perfection is reserved for heaven. In another, it is doing the best we can now with our capacities and circumstances.

My last task in this chapter is to make some proposals about the way in which a Christian may regard phenomena commonly referred to as "mystical" and found in a non-Christian context. It is clear that we cannot confine the life of faith to the visible confines of the Christian church. If anyone wishes to claim that Hindus or Neoplatonists or Sufis or Buddhists are in particular instances showing the signs of the contemplative prayer practised by Christian mystics, there is no reason why they should not be themselves practising this prayer. Whether this is actually the case in any particular instance is another matter on which one may well hesitate to pronounce. For my purposes it does not matter.

What does matter is to realise that phenomena can occur which show superficial if striking resemblances to the phenomena of Christian mysticism and which in fact may have nothing to do with it. Again it is not a question of deciding about particular instances. It is simply a matter of recognising that certain states of mind are possible. It seems to be possible (it is at least conceivable) that there takes place a retirement of the mind within itself such that it is conscious or seems to be conscious of nothing except itself. Christian mystics, among others, have described this state, and they have strongly disapproved of it, although there seems no reason why it *must* lead to trouble. It could be just an agreeable rest from one's usual activities. If it becomes the business of life it certainly deserves disapproval. And if it is supposed to be what all mysticism is, it is a snare and a delusion. It may lead to the worst sort of trouble. It could even stand for the destruction of conscience, the rejection of God. We can only guess at what is really going on. What is undeniable is that it sometimes presents itself as a state of complete fulfilment and that a non-religious account of it can be given.

If we are to take certain descriptions of it at their face-value (and there may be nothing to show that we should not so take them) then we must say that what has emerged is at the furthest extreme from Christian mysticism. It is a concentration on the self and nothing else, a withdrawal of it into itself, whereas Christian mysticism is essentially an outward movement of the self. To repeat, we have to recognise that we cannot rule out such a state of affairs and that it can be a most dangerous one. How are we to explain its startling and apparently beneficent effects? It could be suggested that a mind which becomes transparent to itself naturally has a sense of great fulfilment because a mind is something of great value, and for it to become aware of itself is therefore something great. But the trouble about this is that the mind's greatness is only a potential one. It is capable of true greatness in virtue of an activity coming to it from without. And it is just that which seems to be excluded from the state of affairs which we are now considering. It looks as though we should have to fall back on saying that the mind enjoys a holiday. People who need a holiday are heard to say that they want to do absolutely nothing for a time; and, odd as it may seem to others, they do seem to enjoy it. If they have to spend their working days in continuously disagreeable occupations, then, I suppose, there is immense satisfaction in simply ceasing from them. But this is plainly no sort of fulfilment although it may be accompanied by an affective tone which, like that induced by drugs, may seem like fulfilment. When this state is described as one of "emptiness" this might seem to corroborate the suggestion.

But that expression and others which are equally tricky introduce us to further complications. The Christian mystics talk about "emptiness" too; they are using negative terms as "pointers" to a positive state. Non-Christian writers, then, may sometimes be doing the same thing. And it is often extremely difficult to tell whether they are doing so or not. But it is clear that those who talk about "mystical" knowledge as a kind of self-knowledge are sometimes describing a knowledge of the self which is not just the discovery of the mind as a spiritual principle but a discovery of the self which is felt to be an expansion of it or the discovery of a wider context to which it now seems to belong. There is a sort of "nature-mysticism" in which the self is found as *united* with its natural environment and is sometimes alleged to be *identical* with it. Often it is said to be united or identified with "reality". When negative language is used in such contexts ("emptiness", "nothingness" and so forth), a theist may suspect that it is the sign of an awareness of God.

Here it must be remembered that it can be extremely difficult to characterise an awareness on the basis of the conceptualisations which try to indicate it. A "nature-mystic" who regards theism in general and Christianity in particular as forms of self-deception will avoid the sort of language which religious people use when he refers to his experiences. He will be under the mistaken impression that what they mean by "God" has nothing at all to do with those experiences. If they have an *absolute* quality about them, the theist will want to say, it is because in fact he is in touch with the Absolute and one cannot make sense of an Absolute unless this is the transcendent God. Perhaps this sense of kinship or even of identification with nature is due to the fact that we do *belong* to nature and when we are more fully aware of ourselves we are keenly aware of this also (not just aware *that* it is so). But when this experience has an absolute quality about it, that explanation will not serve.

Again, the non-dualist tradition in the East, touched on in the third chapter, may make the language of union (in place of that of identification) completely unacceptable because it may seem to leave subject and object in an ultimate irreconcilable opposition. The language of subject and object will seem to be peculiarly out of place when we are talking of the Absolute. At this level any sort of distinction is illusory, and to talk about the Absolute as an "object" is in the highest degree improper. One must indeed acknowledge the force in this last objection. What the Christian mystic is talking about would be better expressed by saying that it is conscious union of a being with the Source of being. It is possible that the non-dualist's experience may be properly conceptualisable in just that way, although he may not be ready to accept this. Such conceptualisations are, of course, adopted by some Eastern traditions, but Eastern conceptualisations are commonly very baffling to Westerners since they often appear to contradict one another within the same system. It is too simple, then, to say that we can always distinguish between theist and non-theist systems by discovering whether or not they involve *adoration*. It is sometimes impossible to decide whether they do or not. But there is one commonsense rule which seems pretty reliable : any experience which leads to a proud self-sufficiency and a disregard of others cannot be authentic mysticism; any experience must be of God if it leads to an increase of charity.

There is one theory of "natural mysticism" from which I must dissent, although I cannot claim to be any sort of authority in the field in which its exponents operate. According to this, there is in non-Christian mysticism a union with God "in the order of nature". Whether an individual is capable of it or not is a matter of temperament and training. It is a natural endowment, and in itself it has nothing to do with the life of supernatural faith and charity, although it is the basis on which that life is erected. No doubt a man's psychological make-up will to some extent dispose or indispose him for contemplation. But union with God, according to the theological tradition, is everybody's business. The point, however, which chiefly concerns me here is that a supraconceptual awareness of God is supposed, in this theory, to be present on two levels, natural and supernatural, the latter being reserved, in principle at least, for Christians. A "natural knowledge" of God, I have proposed, is the offer of supernatural life. *Union* with God is always supernatural.

But what of the view that all mysticism is natural, in other words, that in itself it has nothing religious about it and that Christians conceptualise it in their own religious way? The suggestion cannot be directly refuted except by establishing the truth of theism and of Christianity and by a detailed investigation of the facts about Christian living. But it can be pointed out that this theory makes the facts about mysticism singularly hard to explain. For what Christians are supposed to misconstrue is a union with "Being", which, shorn of all religious attributes, seems far too uninteresting to justify all the excitement. That topic and others which have been so hastily touched on in this chapter will receive further treatment in the next.

So far my purpose in this book has been to offer a point of view and a synthesis. I have tried to show how it is possible to give a coherent account of human experience as enlightened by Christian theology but as needing always to be borne in mind by the Christian theologian if what he has to say is to be intelligible. I have made this synthesis as brief as possible, dealing only with such difficulties for one's thought today as arise directly from it, so that it may be considered synoptically, as a conspectus, in all its chief bearings. Hoping to show that there may be a wood to be discerned, I have said little about its trees. And now, to underline the significance of the positions which I have taken up, I start to relate them to those taken up by certain contemporaries. It will be convenient to begin with the topic of mysticism, which has been proposed as central for the whole discussion, so as to develop the lines of thought sketched out in the last chapter.

(i) *F. C. Happold*

His *Mysticism,* published by Penguin Books in 1962, should have done much to encourage the study of mysticism and to increase understanding of it. In comparing his point of view with mine I shall be, of necessity, largely concerned with what seem to me certain shortcomings, and I wish to make it clear at once that I have a sincere admiration for his work.

He begins with a characteristically candid statement of his beliefs. His manuscript, he tells us, was criticised "as having too pronounced a Christian bias", and on this he comments : "If one sincerely believes anything, it is not possible to be coldly objective. Nor is it necessary to be so, provided any bias is frankly acknowledged." That is the spirit in which the present book has been written—but the word "bias" has pejorative implications, and I should prefer to speak here of "conviction" or of "Christian faith". And Happold goes on immediately to mention "faith", but in a way which I find puzzling : "While I am reluctant to apply to Christianity such concepts as 'final' and 'truer than', since neither can be logically demonstrated as valid (they partake of the truth of faith rather than of the truth of reason), I do . . . recognise in Christianity a quality of 'uniqueness' . . ." (p 16). This, on the face of it, may be taken to mean that faith in the Christian revelation ought not to be called an awareness of what is known to be *definitively true* because it cannot be logically demonstrated and that, in so far as the Christian revelation makes its own special claims, these do not represent a valid addition to the truth which is contained in other metaphysical claims. This initial reduction of "truth" to what can be logically demonstrated followed by the suggestion that there is nevertheless something which may be called "the truth of faith" is the first instance of certain incoherence which I find in Happold's statements of his position. It might almost be called characteristic of writers on this subject, and that is why it is worth examining in some detail.

It is, I think, an incoherence which is, on the whole, more apparent than real; but the passage just quoted, coming as it does on the second page of the first chapter, may weigh heavily for a reader and needs to be considered a little further. In the previous paragraph Happold has written that he has "tried to make out a case for regarding the validity of mystical experience and the world-view—the picture of the 'real', which stems from it—as a possible, and not unreasonable, hypothesis". He wants to persuade us, then, that what mysticism is claiming may be quite possibly *true,* although this could not be "logically demonstrated" any more than the claims of Christianity. So there could be no objection *in principle* to someone's putting forward those claims as possibly valid. And therefore to introduce at this point a distinction between "the truth of faith" and "the truth of reason" may suggest that when it comes to specific religious claims we are no longer dealing with questions of objective truth but with subjective interpretations of the "real". In that case we might suppose Happold to think that the Christian one has a "uniqueness" about it only because it has proved fruitful in certain ways. The passage could be easily understood in a familiar syncretist sense, and it does seem to suggest a view of faith as belonging to a sphere beyond that of reason in some anti-intellectualist sense. But I do not at all receive that impression from the book as a whole. It explicitly favours a theistic interpretation as the true one, and there is later on a good deal to suggest that Happold would in fact accept an account of Christian experience as an awareness, an intellection, of what is objectively present. I shall now refer to some relevant passages.

Summing up his discussion of the nature of mysticism, Happold writes of the mystic: "He relies not on deductive reason but on unifying intuitive vision to pierce to the secret. As a result of direct intuitive experience, he finds not only a coherent pattern which is not contrary to his reason, but also a certainty of a sort which cannot be given by philosophy." I think that "direct intuitive experience" is something that a philosopher should be very much concerned with, but otherwise this passage is most acceptable. And a few lines further on, Happold writes : "The sort of knowledge which comes through *intuitus mysticus,* unlike scientific and metaphysical knowledge, has a 'saving' quality; it leads to 'eternal life'. 'This is eternal life', said Jesus, 'to know God and Him whom he has sent' " (p 42). I would not oppose "metaphysical" to "mystical" knowledge in this way, but that is of little consequence here. What Happold asks us to make of mysticism, if we are to regard it seriously (and not as a means of procuring "kicks"), emerges quite clearly in this passage. And the following one is also clear : ". . . while mystical states are akin to states of feeling, they are also states of knowledge. They have a *noetic* quality . . . Even though he may not be able to say, in the language of intellect, what he knows, one who has undergone mystical experience is convinced with absolute certainty that he does know" (p 45).

Unfortunately when Happold pursues the topic of "knowledge", his language is less satisfactory. He begins, promisingly enough, by speaking of a knowledge "based on something which can only be called 'union' " (I have maintained that this is true of our basic experience) and says that "the knowledge which we may have of God is of this sort; but it goes beyond it, for God can only be fully known by *becoming* God . . . and by the self's being taken fully into the divine life and being transformed therein". I have already remarked upon the use of such language by orthodox writers, supported by the Fathers as well as Aristotle, and pointed out that it must not be taken literally. Happold does seem to take it literally, for he continues : "The idea of man *becoming* or being *made* God may be alien to popular conceptions of the nature of God and man, wherein man is thought of as standing over against God" (p 62). The distinction between man and God is indeed often thought of in crude terms, but unless it is preserved the "deification" of man will result either in his abolition in God or in reducing God to man's changing condition (God will "develop" by *adding* man to himself). The discovery of the Infinite as *beyond* the finite is the basis of empirical theism.

The trouble seems to be caused, in part, by a recurrent tendency to make mystical knowledge so remote from our ordinary experience that it can be referred to only in paradoxical terms. There is nothing really paradoxical about saying that God is inexpressible and that we are only what we receive (the two statements which are fundamental for mysticism). But to say that the knowledge of God has nothing to do with our normal ways of knowing is unnecessarily off-putting. According to Happold, the mystics "are compelled to say that, in terms of the intellect, God, since he cannot be comprehended by the rational faculty, is unknown and unknowable". The operative phrase here is "in terms of the intellect", for the passage continues : "That, however, is only part of the story. Though unknown and unknowable by the intellect, by what Dionysius the Areopagite calls the *higher faculty,* it is possible for man to be united 'to Him who is wholly unknowable; thus by knowing nothing he knows that which is beyond his knowledge' " (p 63). The Areopagite is only saying in a paradoxical way that God and our knowledge of him are ineffable, inexpressible—which is in itself a perfectly intelligible notion to anyone who, for example, has tried to put into words the *beauty* of a sonata or a sonnet. My point is not just that it is a pity to use "intellect" as the equivalent of discursive reason when it means, in traditional usage, "intelligent intuition" (Happold, like so many writers, frequently opposes it to "intuition") but that this reference to a union brought about by a "higher faculty" may suggest that we are being invited to give up *intelligibility* altogether. And in that case we can say that God is distinct from the soul and that he is not, or that we are aware of him and that we are not aware of him and expect to get away with it.

That is precisely what seems to happen at times in Happold's book. I should like to think that he is only reporting the views of others when he makes these unintelligible statements, but the passages already quoted make it difficult to do so. He writes of the "Atman" in Hindu thought : "This self is present in all, yet distinct from all. It is a Universal Self and at the same time a personal Self . . . there is nothing in the world that it not God." And he also quotes here : "The knowledge that Brahman (God) and Atman (the divine Self in man) are one and the same is true knowledge." This is followed by an explanation of *maya* : "In general it is used to indicate the tendency to identify ourselves with our apparent selves and an apparent universe, to be deceived by the appearance which conceals the reality. It does not mean that the empirical world and the selves in it are mere illusion or are not, in their way, real; it means that they are not seen as, in their essential nature, they really are" (pp 107-8), at which point Happold makes his comment

on all this: "It was a magnificent achievement in spiritual understanding." He then discusses the charge of "exaggerated other-
worldliness" brought against Hindu thought, but does not appear
to find any other difficulties in it. Yet some of the sentences just
quoted plainly contradict one another: God is said to be both
distinct from the world and not distinct from it; everything is really
one and yet there is something called "illusion" which is not part
of it. And it will be recalled that in an earlier passage Happold
spoke of the mystic as one who finds "a coherent pattern which is
not contrary to his reason . . ." One is reminded of the contradictions enunciated by some of the British Hegelians who flourished
in our universities at the beginning of the century.

In making these criticisms it is Happold's own attitude to Hindu
thought with which I am concerned rather than Hindu thought
itself. Orientals have their traditional ways of speaking, and it is not
to be expected that they will change them because they are baffling
to us. Sometimes we can satisfy ourselves, I think, that they and we
are talking about the same thing; sometimes we have to conclude
that they are talking about something else—and we cannot reach
our conclusion solely on the basis of a logical analysis of what they
say. It is tempting to interpret what they say about *maya* as pointing to the true nature of created things as deriving from their
infinite source (a "positivist" view of them being a myopic one);
but a reference to "creation" would be rejected by them for reasons
on which I have touched already (in the third chapter) in connection with "non-dualism", a doctrine which Happold has *seemed*
to find unexceptionable, at least to the extent that man is *eventually*
identified with God. But that *some* sort of dualism is unavoidable is
surely clear from the fact that there are illusions to be dispersed.
The point has been made often enough, but it leaves "non-dualists"
unmoved.

Happold lumps together experiences which may need to be distinguished. He quotes, for example, the famous passage in Saint
Augustine's *Confessions* (book VII) in which he speaks of beholding the "Light Unchangeable" and speaks of it as "above my sou'.,
because it made me"; and he then quotes a typical instance of
nature-mysticism from Anya Seton's *The Winthrop Woman* at the
climax of which we find: "She felt love pouring from the light . . .
the love was far off at the source of the light, and yet it drenched
her through. And the source and she were one." Certainly it is not
easy to explain that experience in a non-theistic way, but we can-

not safely identify it, as it stands, with Augustine's experience, in which dependence on the source is emphasised and in which there are moral implications. Happold regards both as examples of "a new vision of the phenomenal world" which is "essentially one of Immanence, of the One, however the One may be conceived, present and permeating the All". He may be right. But his comment is nevertheless disquieting : "Here all the chief characteristics of the *pan-en-henic* experience are present, the perception of the *fusion* [my italics] of the One in the All, and the All in the One . . ." (p 91).

Despite such ambiguities and apparent confusions (and one could quote many more) I am still left with the impression that Happold would not dispute what Saint John of the Cross says of "deification" in this passage which he quotes from *The Spiritual Canticle* : "Then the natures are so united, what is divine so communicated . . . that, *without undergoing any essential change each seems to be God . . .*" (p 99). And on the same page we find the admission : "Among the Christian mystics, though the language used sometimes seems to carry a different meaning, an essential 'otherness' between God and the creature is always maintained." In his account of Eckhart he had described him as "uncertain" on this point (p 49); if he is now suggesting that the uncertainty is in Eckhart's language rather than in his thought, he is in line with the most recent scholarship on the subject. I mention this here because an appeal to Eckhart has been such a regular feature of vaguely pantheistic writings.

Happold's book is important not only as one which has had a wide circulation but also as one which has shown in a most persuasive way what he rightly describes as "a most impressive basic unanimity" among mystical writers of any substance : "it is difficult to escape the conclusion that all have glimpsed in varying degrees and in varying forms the same Reality and found the same Truth" (p 118). It may seem curious that he should make no mention here of Bergson, who was brought to the acceptance of Christianity by reaching that same conclusion. But the moving testimony with which he ends his account makes the genuineness of his own belief, whatever theoretical confusions it may involve, abundantly clear : "There are times when the awakened soul, craving for a revelation which will make sense of the riddle of the universe, of the apparent futility of life, and of its own inadequacy, may feel that there is no answer. Sick with longing, it can only cry *'De profundis, Domine'*. But the desire is everything; for the prayer of desire is not seldom the prelude of the revelation. Suddenly 'the timeless moment' is there, the morning stars sing together, a sense of utter joy, utter certainty, and utter unworthiness mingle, and in awe and wonder it murmurs 'I know'."

(ii) *William Johnston, S.J.*

In *The Absolute and the Atonement* I discussed Fr Johnston's book *The Mysticism of "The Cloud of Unknowing"* and mingled praise of it with certain complaints about what are, from my point of view, its relapses into a conventional theology which I believe to have had its day. Since then another book of his, *The Still Point* (Fordham University Press, 1970), has come into my hands. It is described as a series of "reflections on Zen and Christian Mysticism", and a brief discussion of its principal themes will bring us back to the topics adumbrated at the end of the last chapter. The difficulties which I felt about the earlier book are less in evidence, and the sympathetic approach to Zen in these pages may prove to be of importance for the "Zen-Christian dialogue". Fr Johnston took part in the meeting of 1968 at Kyoto, at which Buddhists and Christians found, he tells us, that what united them was "not philosophy but religious experience". He explains : "While in philosophical formulations we were poles apart, when it came to the discussion of values we were one." One sees what he means, yet I should wish to add that if we treat philosophy and religious experience as wholly distinct topics the dialogue will never face the real issue. Mr Happold, in the book just discussed, distinguishes three kinds of mysticism : "soul-mysticism", "nature-mysticism" and "God-mysticism". The problem, for a Christian, is to account for the first two of these mysticisms. Are they always to be reduced to the third in some way when their results are not only beneficial but spiritually impressive? Or is there some further factor involved in such cases which is not explicable in religious terms at all?

No-one who reads what Johnston has to say in his first chapter about Zen *satori* can doubt that it must be taken very seriously. Sometimes, after "a tremendous effort of mind and body . . . in a moment, everything unifies and enlightenment comes as an enormously joyful relief. The experience is followed by calm, joy, interior freedom and detachment : it gives that liberty from the shackles of worldly desire which, says Buddhism, is the source of

all our suffering". Johnston goes on to speak of "other enlighten-
ments which are more quietly spiritual, prompted by an aesthetic
experience and penetrating deeply into the personality" (pp 12-13).
He remarks that "it is extremely difficult to find infallible
norms to judge the validity of intuitive experiences" (p 15), but
it is also extremely difficult, it seems to me, for a Christian to conclude that those just described can be given a non-theistic explanation.

Johnston does not raise the question at once, but turns in his
second chapter to Christian mystical experience. Here, I was glad
to see, he remarks that "many theologians hold that Christian
mysticism is no more than an intensification of the ordinary Christian life . . . a deepening of that faith and love that every true
Christian possesses", so that "every convinced Christian is a mystic
in embryo; he already possesses a touch of Christian *samadhi* and is
on his way to an enlightenment which may only reach its perfection after death" (pp 26-7). Equally satisfactory is the conclusion :
"Empty of conceptual knowledge, the soul is filled with supraconceptual wisdom; poor in images and ideas, it is rich in superior
knowledge of God." The passage, however, continues : "And this
mystical wisdom comes from charity. We know that in our ordinary
lives, sympathy gives deep insight into the hearts of those we love;
and it is the same in things divine" (p 31). Here we find the familiar
suggestion that love can itself provide knowledge and that this is
the hall-mark of Christian mysticism, distinguishing it from other
kinds. This seems to be a misunderstanding of the fact that the
growth of knowledge is *conditioned* by love. Later, as in his earlier
book, Johnston recognises that knowledge and love are bound up
with one another, when they are exercised with any fullness, in such
sort that it becomes hard to make any distinction between them.
A knowledge which can arouse little interest is a shallow sort of
knowledge; a love which does not fully respond to an offer is an
incomplete love; a love which exhausts itself upon an unworthy
object is a disordered love. Union is a loving knowledge or an intelligent love.

When Johnston goes on to speak of union with God he speaks of
"the destruction of subject-object relationship" in Christian
mysticism and says that it is "different from Zen" not only because
it is "a union of love" but also because "while Zen is sometimes
called a meditation without an object, the author of *The Cloud*
speaks of meditation without a subject". And he adds : "Nor is

this distinction merely one of semantics. To forget self so that only God remains is different from forgetting everything until only self remains" (p 38). Two comments are called for. If the subject of the Christian experience is supposed to have actually disappeared (as opposed to being absorbed, psychologically, in God), then Christian mystics would indeed be saying just what so many Eastern mystics seem to say. But they certainly do not *mean* that. We also gather that Zen, in so far as it is called "meditation without an object", is in fact nothing but the awareness of the self, and we should then want to know what is this "self" which is the source of such spiritual riches. But these remarks of Johnston's are by no means his last words on the subject. At the end of this same second chapter, in a valuable account of the Trinitarian character of Christian mysticism (there is "an element of diversity or separation within the very unity" in this "unitive prayer"), he speaks of Saint Teresa's description of the seventh mansion and comments : "There is no doubt here about the unity and separation : union and separation between the Persons of the Trinity, union and separation between Teresa and her God" (p 41). That, I would say, makes good sense. So it seems a pity that Johnston should bring this discussion to a close with a reference to "paradoxes" which will "never be solved"—mysteries, in the theological sense, I prefer to say, which will never be exhausted.

In the third chapter we come to Jung's proposal that "Zen makes the unconscious conscious, leading to an integration of the whole personality . . ." (p 48). No doubt the abolishing of unconscious conflicts by means of psychoanalysis can have most satisfactory results. It may even be the necessary preliminary to an awareness of God's action upon the soul. But it does not seem to be of itself a sufficient explanation of *satori*. Talk of the "untapped realms of the psyche" and of the "treasures in the unconscious" is not easy to interpret, for Jung is notoriously not an exact thinker. Johnston's interest in all this is that it "points to the fact that an experience beyond subject and object is a reality which cannot be denied", and he holds that the experience of Christian mystics and Zen monks have something in common (p 51). That is to say, there is a unitive experience in each case but the cause of it (and therefore its meaning, its significance and its value) is not the same in each case. But are we to conclude that knowledge of the self alone and knowledge of God in the self are experientially the same although ontologically different?

Johnston touches on that question in his fourth chapter, when he speaks of "grace"; "its presence is known chiefly by faith and studied by the theologian" (p 62). It is certainly true, as he goes on to say, that supernatural grace cannot be observed "under the microscope of clinical psychology", but that is because, in the sense which Johnston seems to be assigning to it, it does not exist at all. It is not a supernatural entity distinct from both God and the soul but a relationship in which they stand. And to suggest that no one can be aware of this relationship, except in very peculiar circumstances, is, as I have tried to show, to make nonsense of the theology of faith. What seems to lie behind the theological slogan that grace is unobservable is the fact that nobody can be certain while he is still in this world that he might not be led to abandon God —in that sense, nobody can be "assured of salvation"; but it is quite another thing to say that nobody can know here and now whether he is accepting God's summons or not. "Besides", Johnston continues, "it would be theologically erroneous to exclude the presence of grace in non-Christian mysticism" (that is, in a non-Christian *context*, for there is no non-Christian grace). But this is not to the point when we are asking how to account for phenomena which resemble those found in Christian mysticism but seem to resist explanation in Christian terms. It may be added that Zennists will be reasonably put off by something called "grace" of which normally nobody can be conscious. It is in the course of this same account of the "psychological structure" of Christian mysticism that Johnston describes "the deepest prayer" as an "ineffable stirring in the deepest centre of one's being that can scarcely be called either knowledge or love, for it is a delicate blend of both" (p 64). So now we can breathe more freely.

And a little later we can breathe still more freely when we find the clear statement that the Christian mystics "are attempting to express not only their moments of highest experience but also the knowledge they have from faith and reason . . . they are eschewing any form of pantheism, any indication that the 'ego' may be an utterly illusory thing" (p 70). But it is surely not the case that they have always to *correct* these "moments of highest experience" by knowledge derived from other sources. The Christian's awareness of God has always the same ontological structure which will not be misconceived except by those who unwittingly bring to it philosophical presuppositions of a kind which leads them to talk nonsense. And one cannot help adopting in practice some philosophical attitude in these matters if one is to speak of them at all. Significantly, Johnston speaks of "paradox" again : "the tremendous paradox of how one can become the other while remaining oneself . . ." (p 71). That, if I may repeat it once more, is just the fact of knowledge with which the philosopher should start.

Johnston seems to be coming back to the real problem when he speaks of the "deep virtue" of the Zen masters : "one cannot but wonder where these virtues come from" (p 97), and the answer which he eventually offers is that the "silence of mysticism", which must here refer to both Christian mysticism and Zen, effects "a certain deep detachment which, in turn, leads to love" (p 105); he has remarked, shortly before, that "in Buddhism generally, the element of positive love is less conspicuous : but that it is not completely absent is clear from the gratitude and kindness of those who have persevered to the peak-point of *satori*". The conclusion to which a Christian must come is presumably that *satori* is the discovery and acceptance of God in the self. Silence, in this context, *is* a detachment from everything except the "ground" of the soul, and the question arises whether this detachment deserves the name of "mystical" *unless* it issues in the discovery and the acceptance of God. It may produce psychological integration and remove certain disorders, but if it does no more than that it is fundamentally different from theistic experience. Johnston accepts that "the detachment attained to in Zen and Yoga has been used to deaden the moral conscience . . ." (p 108). His account of "detachment" in terms of "psychological growth" (p 101), although it is only a condition, not the cause, of theistic experience, nevertheless suggests a possible answer to the question which I have found so difficult : why does a detachment which is apparently quite atheistic have such startling and beneficial results? An abrupt restoration to that psychological *health* which seems to be the necessary preliminary to "growth" could be the explanation.

Later on Johnston does himself advance, hesitantly, and in a curiously casual way, the proposal which I have just recommended about *satori* : "The Zennist . . . does not profess any dependence on a deity . . . But I wonder if what he has reached in *satori* is a pure consciousness of dependence (or a consciousness of pure dependence) without a knowledge of what is depended upon. If one were to say that the Zen contemplative is, in the last analysis, looking for what Christians call God, most Zen people would reject outright this way of speaking. Yet one cannot but wonder if they are not seeking something upon which it is impossible to put any name except that of God" (pp 116-17). It seems to me that unless Christians fully accept the existence of anonymous theism their claims for Christianity as the definitive religion will seem quite implausible in the eyes of intelligent non-Christians. What else except God can one suppose to be "contemplated" after this fashion?

Unfortunately Johnston takes the edge off that passage by what follows : "The Christian mystics often speak of God in terms very reminiscent of Zen . . . Perhaps they, too, attain to a consciousness of pure dependence; and only dark faith gives them the knowledge that what they depend on is the transcendent God who can only be 'known by unknowing', who can be loved but not known." It is surely quite obvious that Christian mystics "attain to a consciousness of pure dependence", and this, as Johnston himself has said, must be called knowledge as well as love. But what is particularly unfortunate about this passage is that he may seem here to be treating "dark faith" as something wholly *extraneous* to this consciousness; yet, it will be recalled, he has referred, with apparent approval, to the traditional doctrine that faith is the "seed" of mystical knowledge.

What he proceeds to say about faith confirms this unfortunate impression. He raises the question whether "the inner certainty of being loved once for all can be acquired". And his answer is : "It is tempting to say that the Christian faith provides such certainty by its assurance of God's immense love. Yet I cannot confidently assert this." Man, he tells us, "may, of course, know by faith that God loves him once for all; and he may believe this with all his being. But faith is faith : it is not vision; it is 'dark'; it inevitably contains what theologians now call the 'element of risk' " (p 119). Christian faith, I have maintained, although it remains at risk, contains an element of vision; it does not just inform us of God's immense love—it puts us in touch with it, and can make us *certain* of it. What else can it mean to say that a man "may believe this with all his being"?

The difference between Johnston's position and mine becomes increasingly marked as the book proceeds. He lays it down that Christianity "though it contains a strong current of mysticism, is not essentially mystical" for "traditionally, mysticism is valued only as a means to something more important—namely, the charity which is the centre of the Gospel message" (p 123). Is there, then, something found in Christianity which deserves to be called mysticism and is not itself an exercise of loving faith? Is not mysticism itself the knowledge and the love of God and of all his creation? Johnston does add that "deep contemplative prayer is indeed a way (and perhaps the best way) to Christian charity", but is it not traditional teaching that such prayer is itself an act of charity— and of charity in an eminent degree?

The workings of Johnston's mind are revealed to us when he takes over as a definition of mysticism Saint Thomas's definition of *contemplatio* : "a simple intuition of the truth". This definition, he tells us, can be applied "to the Zen *satori* and to any other religious or philosophical experience which genuinely grasps the truth" (p 127). What truth? The contents of the "cavernous depths" of the mind so often appealed to in the book? And, if so, just what are they? Or does a genuine grasp of the truth mean (as it should do) knowledge of God? We must suppose so. And then what is the difference between Christian and non-Christian mysticism? Johnston answers, as on a previous occasion, by distinguishing the former as that "which arises from, and culminates in, love of God in Christ' '(p 129). The other sort of mysticism is a "simple intuition of the truth" and nothing more. So it is mysticism in that latter sense which is "only a means for something more important". We may still wonder how Christianity is intelligible without this intuition, which was said to be not of its essence, but at least we now seem to have discovered Johnston's doctrine of mysticism. Christian mysticism (which, he allows, is not confined to professing Christians) is inspired by the love of God; there is also a mysticism which is simply an awareness of him.

Is this acceptable? I cannot think so. When there is awareness of God, we either turn away from it altogether (and then, of course, it goes underground) or we accept it, and even if we are not wholehearted about it we have some love of God. The psychological conditions which can be brought about automatically by the use of techniques or drugs are another matter altogether; they should not be lumped together with the apprehension of God under a single name. Let us conclude by accepting Johnston's remark, in reference to drugs, that "the *true* [my italics] mystical descent to the core of one's being is always accompanied by progress in moral virtue and in psychic maturity, and it effects a reform or conversion or whatever it may be" (p 138). That can have, I think, only one reasonable explanation.

(iii) *Wilbur Marshall Urban*

Someone might comment that the two books which I have discussed were not written by "thinkers", if by "thinkers" we mean
"professional philosophers". I should not equate the terms myself,
but in any case English-speaking philosophers do not concern themselves much with mysticism. When they do it is usually to insist that
mysticism can never *prove* anything. And positivists who warn us
against the absurdities of Plato and who have read, apparently, only
a few extracts, will sometimes make general statements about mysticism on the basis of a nodding acquaintance with (say) Plotinus and
Eckhart. Exceptions, however, do occur, and I shall mention one
of them which I have only just now encountered, although the
book in question was published over twenty years ago. The late
Professor W. M. Urban's *Humanity and Deity* (Allen and Unwin)
ends with a chapter on mysticism which is, for the most part,
extremely welcome and brings out certain aspects of the topic on
which I have touched so far only lightly.

He considers mysticism to be "an essential element in all religious
experience and its expression"; if we take it "in the broadest sense",
it is "not only the mother-sea and fountain-head of all religion,
but also an essential element in all discourse about God". Both
"positive" and "negative" theology presuppose "an element of
mysticism". For "if God can be named, if by analogy we can apply
to Him, the unconditioned, our predicates as humanly conditioned,
we must also know, in some fashion at least, what it is in Him that
makes possible . . . their application in a supereminent degree". And
if we say that God cannot be named, "to know that He cannot we
must also know what it is in Him that makes our names inapplic-
able" (pp 427-8). That is what I have been saying. It should help to
make clear that "positive" and "negative" theology are two
elements of a single process in which God is discovered "beyond"
the finite as its source.

That is, I think, the truth in Urban's main contention that
mysticism has "everything to do with symbols". For it is a "height-
ened noesis" which occurs "with and through the images and
symbols" and "we must seek to understand it and evaluate it in the
context of our human knowledge as a whole" (pp 428-9). It is
through the finite that we find God. But Urban insists that in
doing so we do not leave "images and symbols" behind; we continue all the time to make conscious use of them : "Even in the

mystical experience the symbol is part of the intuition itself",
although "in some forms of mysticism the symbol is in the end
negated"—not, however, in the "major forms" (p 430). The great
mystics would not agree. Nor would those who speak of the way in
which an aesthetic experience may lead to a "take-off" in which
the music or whatever it may be ceases to be an object of attention
at all and a purely apophatic experience supervenes. Urban appeals
to Saint Thomas's doctrine that all human knowledge in this life
is based on "phantasms". "We may be sure", he says, "that in principle the contention is sound" (p 447). It may be right to say that
mystical knowledge is always *accompanied* by phantasms (it has
been authoritatively maintained that, although the mystics do not
advert to them, there must be in fact some *production* of "images"
in the sensibility), but there does not seem to be ground for maintaining that "images" are the indispensable *medium* in which God is
found. There is, however, no need to hesitate about the conclusion
which Urban draws at this point : "Even mystical experience of
God cannot be wholly unmediated." For it is always mediated by
self-knowledge, if by nothing else.

What is perhaps most valuable about Urban's account is his
insistence that mysticism *is* an affair of knowledge, and must therefore be understood as being in continuity with what we mean by
knowledge in the ordinary way : "It is only because mysticism *eo
nomine* is but a specialised form of all human consciousness that
what the mystics tell us can be understood . . . the situation is
similar to that of natural and supernatural faith. If we envisage the
latter as something wholly unrelated to the natural and primary
acknowledgements of value characteristic of moral consciousness,
we end in making it wholly unintelligible. The same is true of any
complete divorce between natural and theological mysticism"
(pp 434-5). My vocabulary is rather different, and I should want
to say that "natural faith" and "natural mysticism" are themselves
theological, although not explicitly so. Apart from this, the passage expresses in an effective way one of the principal contentions
of these chapters.

Urban emphasises the "humanity" of the main stream of Christian mysticism. The recognition of God's creatures as "reflections"
of him on which I have laid stress is here shown to be specially
characteristic of the mystics, although they may speak of it in their
own ways : "The language which the mystics speak is, in the first
instance at least, the language of poetry, as all religious language

is, and, as we are told, 'wholly concrete'. Its images and symbols are taken, in the main, from sources so deep in the human heart that they are understandable to all those for whom the heart has a language which the intellect knows not of"—but the contrast here, in its traditional form, is that between the "heart" or *intellect* and the *reason*. And after referring to *The Song of Songs* Urban points out that "there is also the love of the creature for all created things and this also may be a natural analogue . . . 'The flower garden of the world', is, for the mystic, 'the veritable clothing of God' " (p 438). Hence, Urban remarks, the exuberance of the language of the mystics; it expresses "the fusion of value with being which is the essential note of mysticism" (p 440).

Urban's emphasis on this "essential note" is most important. "The really fundamental character of all mystics", he writes, "is . . . that they are able to make certain syntheses which the non-mystical find impossible." He instances, among others, the synthesis of perfect activity and perfect repose, and continues : "Above all there is the synthesis of the One and the Good—of the *ens perfectissimum* and the *ens realissimum*. The essence of mysticism is then the *coincidentia oppositorium* which, on the intellectual side at least, has been the *sine qua non* of mysticism of all times and all places" (p 431). The synthesis of perfect activity and perfect repose may be called a synthesis of apparent opposites, although even in our experience of ourselves we can sometimes find ourselves *dwelling upon* something in a condition which we might want to describe as one of reposeful activity. But the synthesis of the One and the Good is surely not one of *opposites* at all. Nevertheless it is certainly one which people can fail to make. Urban goes on to say that the "fusion of the Good or Value with Being" is the synthesis "about which all the others revolve". He insists upon it again and again : "It is this blending . . . that constitutes the final insight of all great religion and great philosophy alike . . . 'The One or the Good', the title of the sixth Ennead of Plotinus, represents the highest expression of natural mysticism and the identity of the Good with Being the highest form of theological mysticism" (pp 431-2). This underlines in a striking way my contention that there is a "metaphysical" meaning for "good" and that one's whole approach to ethics depends upon whether one recognises it or not.

This might seem to make discussion on that subject of little use. But it must be remembered that Urban regards mystical knowledge as being in continuity with ordinary knowledge. And the passage last quoted continues : "The deliverances of reason may indeed lead us to the insight that *ens et bonum convertuntur,* but the full realisation of the actuality of the synthesis is itself possible only by trenching upon the mystical." I doubt whether "reason" has much to do with it. What it amounts to, I believe, is simply the conclusion that an awareness of God lies at the heart of our experience. All one can do is to use whatever means there may be at hand to educe it. As Urban observes later, "logic can give us merely correctness and not truth . . . unless thought can conceive from some other source it remains lifeless and barren" (p 449).

After his discussion of this "central synthesis" Urban proceeds to mention others, one of which, he says, "stands out as of primary importance and of equal significance for mystical theology, namely, the synthesis of the temporal with the timeless". He comments : "The dualism of time and eternity . . . is for thought alone perhaps unsolvable"—naturally, one must remark, if it is a matter not just of "thought" but of apprehension. Later he returns to the topic and in this connection his remarks are especially welcome. He quotes from the *Thirty Nine Articles* of the Church of England : "There is but one living and true God, everlasting, without parts and passions . . ." (this, as he says, is the voice of "all traditional theology"), and he goes on : "Without passions as well as without parts—non-temporal as well as non-spatial. Nor is there any question what has driven religious thought to this belief in the Divine impassibility. It is the underlying assumption that a Being must exist to whom nothing may attach which could present itself to thought as an imperfection; only a most perfect Being can, for religious thought—and ultimately for religious feeling also—be called God" (p 454). And after a discussion of current objections, closely in line with my own discussion of them in an earlier chapter, he concludes, as I concluded, "it does not follow at all that although the Divine life cannot be *imagined* apart from time, it cannot, and must not, be *thought* as timeless" (p 456). This may serve as an introduction to the next chapter.

Urban's book was published when metaphysics was even less popular among us than it is today. With all its prolixities and incidental shortcomings (among which I would myself include a misconception of the relationship of intuition with its expression), it is an imposing witness to the great tradition of metaphysical thought. Perhaps it may become better appreciated in our own time.

It might be expected that I should discuss here in some detail the anthropomorphic way in which so many modern philosophers treat of God, the ignorance which they often show of the claims which they are purporting to refute, the various philosophical prejudices which prevent them from appreciating these claims even when they are aware of them and their attempts to show that the facts to which religious apologists appeal can be satisfactorily explained in naturalistic terms. But I am not proposing to go over ground which I have already covered in principle, very rapidly indeed in the present book and at greater length in others, except in so far as my discussions in this chapter of three contemporary writers may involve some brief reference to one or other of these topics. The central issue, as I see it, is always whether in fact there is something in human experience which can reveal itself to us as a contact with what is other than ourselves and to which we are bound if we are to achieve ourselves, this presenting itself to us as both completely beyond us and at the same time absolutely necessary to us. Do we or do we not find ourselves in a situation which can be indicated only by the use of such language?

(i) *Thomas McPherson*

Professor McPherson's book, entitled *The Philosophy of Religion,* published in 1965, has many merits. It is straightforward and readable, and it clears up a number of confusions in a useful way. So it is a rather ungrateful task to pick out the main points of disagreement. To do this, however, will, I think, help to explain the importance which I attach to certain contentions.

On his first page McPherson writes: "What I am attempting in this book is some clarification of certain concepts and arguments." This may already suggest that he does not regard appeals to experience as of the first importance for the philosophy of religion, and we shall see that this is in fact the case. What he considers its "central theme", he tells us on the next page, is "the place of reason in religion". Philosophy is of course concerned with logical processes, but I have contended that it should be concerned in the first place with the fundamental human awareness which logical processes presuppose. Its business is clarification, but clarification in the first place of that awareness. And that clarification is not itself, fundamentally, a logical process but results from a persevering *attention*. McPherson does not adopt that point of view. It is one which contemporary English-speaking philosophers very seldom adopt. It has nothing to do with "a strong tendency at the present time to describe religion as non-rational or irrational" (p 6) because it does not reject logic. What is illogical is always untrue. And logic has its indispensable uses. But whether, for example, I am at the mercy of my character and my circumstances up to date so that I can now "choose" only as they dictate to me—this is not to be decided by an appeal to logic. My awareness of moral freedom is a matter of fact.

On the one hand, then, I am in entire agreement with McPherson when, in the course of his discussion of the "traditional" arguments for God, he points out that, since Thomists do not allow us "direct" knowledge of him, "an element of inference, of some kind or other, must come into our knowledge of him" and that if they also admit that their own "cosmological" argument is not a strict one, there is "a certain conflict in the Thomist position" (p 60). The argument is certainly not a strict one, as McPherson goes on at once to say, for everything depends on seeing that the world is "finite" in a sense which, if it means anything to the purpose, means that it cannot account for its own existence, and nobody who is not already prepared to acknowledge God is going to acknowledge that. (It can always be said, without contradiction, that no question of accounting for the world's existence need arise.) McPherson says rightly that we are being asked to detect in the world "a feature called the feature of being finite" and then "to take the step of inferring from this to an Infinite Being as the necessary ground of the finite world". Clearly we cannot do this.

On the other hand, there can be evidence for God, I have claimed, which without involving any illogicality (without contradicting what we already know or leading to a contradiction) is not itself the result of a logical process, and McPherson does not favour this approach. When he discusses the moral evidence for God, he discusses the contention that "the absoluteness of moral principles can only be guaranteed if they are somehow derived from the will of God" (p 97) and concludes that it depends upon the confused notion that a moral rule which is absolute in the sense of admitting of no exception must have its *origin* in the Absolute. But the moral evidence for God, as I see it, is not of that kind. My claim is that we can be aware of powers which we *ought* absolutely to actualise and that this is a summons to fulfilment which is at the same time a demand for *acceptance* : this is an awareness or experience of God.

Before coming to McPherson's comments on appeals to experience we may pause to note his comments on the question : "Is not God worshipped as all-good, so that his will, unlike that of any other being, always issues in decisions and commands that are good . . . ?" The passage reads as follows :

> . . . we must reply that, although God is worshipped as all-good, this does not rule out the possibility of his being supposed evil on at least some occasions. ("God is good" is not usually taken as analytic : at least, no reputable theologian has ever, so far as I know, treated it as if it were.) Indeed, it is just this possibility which is one of the things that goes to make the problem of Evil . . . such a serious difficulty for the reflective religious believer. It seems to me, though this might be disputed, to be a matter of contingent fact, not a matter of necessity, that God's will is always good (p 99).

McPherson adds that otherwise "God is good" is "probably vacuous".

These remarks astonish me. "God" in our society normally means the Father of Jesus Christ, and it should not be necessary to say that the Christian tradition identifies God and absolute goodness. It is, I have maintained, *as* absolute goodness that we originally discover him. It is true that an obsolete natural theology claimed to demonstrate the "existence" of a First Cause and then to deduce God's "nature" and "attributes", but it is not the case that the Christian knowledge of God rests upon such a foundation. And the problem of evil, for an intelligent theist, is not a problem about the nature of God, but one of reconciling what happens in the world with his goodness. If there is a demonstrable contradiction here (as McPherson seems later to conclude) then the theist can be an honest theist no longer. Behind all this is McPherson's subscription to the view that morality is independent of religion and indeed superior to it on the ground that we can rightly obey God's commands only if we think that they are right. To this my reply is that for the Christian metaphysican the standard of goodness *is* God. What others may call an independent, impersonal, moral absolute the Christian identifies with infinite goodness, the supra-personal source of finite goodness. That is why "God is good" is not "probably vacuous", although it is a statement which it should not be necessary to make.

I now turn to McPherson's chapter on "religious experience". He points out that the topic is "largely post-Romantic Revolution", adding that "an appeal to religious experience in the proof of God's existence is something that would not have occurred to Anselm or Aquinas, or even Descartes" (p 101). It might be supposed that I should find this a very awkward fact. I have indeed been concerned to point out that the directness of our knowledge of God, its experimental character, is something which scholastic theologians have tended to overlook. But this does not at all incline me to suppose that the faithful (including these theologians) have been without this awareness of God down the centuries. Evidence to the contrary is overwhelming (unless of course it all can be written off as "pathological"). During the "Christian centuries" the affirmation of God was taken pretty well for granted, so it was not something which theologians had to take very seriously. (Presumably that is why Saint Thomas's "proofs" are somewhat perfunctory.) And when they did have to face up to the question, it was natural for them to try to tackle their adversaries, as far as they could, on the common ground of sense-experience and logical procedures. To suppose that you can "prove God" and then to find that your conviction rests in fact on a deeper foundation than you supposed is probably quite a common experience. The faithful at large have not concerned themselves much with reasonings about it, and if these were essential to religion only a small minority could have been religious. Some may have been persuaded that they had been performing a "spontaneous inference", but if they had subsequently discovered that this could not be the explanation (since no valid inferential process can in fact be exhibited) I doubt whether they would have been much perturbed.

But the real question is whether the appeal to religious experience is a valid one. That depends on what you mean by it. McPherson goes on to tell us that it "means some kind of emotional experience or condition, or an experience or condition that is somehow both emotional and cognitive". As a statement about common usage that is undeniable. But I have pointed out that the Christian tradition claims a knowledge of God which must be understood, I hold, as a cognitive experience (which has, like all experience, an affective tone). One cannot be forbidden to call this "religious experience" on the grounds that this expression has a predominantly emotional connotation in the popular mind. McPherson does indeed allow that it might be used to mean a "direct acquaintance with God", but this "is generally considered to be essentially inner or private—and even, it is sometimes added, incommunicable" (p 103). Put like that, it does sound like some purely personal idiosyncrasy. Here I must refer to what I have already said about the unspectacular character of the "direct acquaintance with God" which I think to be at the root of all human knowledge; and to the fact that no experience can be directly communicated from one person to another. I could not directly communicate to you my knowledge of a mutual friend, my experiences of hearing his voice, for instance, and my understanding of his words, but we should not doubt that our experiences of this kind were in principle and in normal circumstances substantially the same for both of us. And the fact that I cannot directly communicate my experience to somebody else is no reason at all for concluding that I cannot rely on it myself. Here we meet a Wittgensteinian prejudice against "inner objects".

McPherson, in this connexion, contrasts the appeal to personal experience with "something that might be called the experience of the Church, which the individual may take over and enter into". Learning from other people is indeed a way of broadening one's own experience. And Christians share in the experience of Christ. But it has to become their *own* experience. They can rely on its report only if they are seeing something *for themselves.* Even when we can rely absolutely on an authority without making another's experience our own, we have to *see,* as I have emphasised earlier, the reliability of that authority, and this means that we must have a direct acquaintance with it, recognising it as an authority. In fact we must be aware of God as authorising us to believe what he reveals to us. McPherson refers throughout to the "Private Experience View" in a derogatory way on the Wittgensteinian ground that *knowledge* can be properly claimed only in so far as we are using publicly observable criteria.

So naturally at the end of this chapter we find the notion that a self-authenticating experience does not make sense. McPherson first asks : how does such a notion help other people in their doubts? The answer is that the claim to such experience is not intended directly to do so. But a person who makes that claim is qualified to help by explaining how he came to have the experience and how, therefore, his interlocutor may hope to have it. And the doubts can be in fact removed in this way. More fundamentally McPherson produces the familiar objection that this is of no help even to the claimant: "Just to feel that something is the case, just to have an intuition that matters are so-and-so, is not to have a reason" (p 117). "Intuitions" are allowed, but they always require to be backed up and justified by reasons. "The intuitionist as much as anyone else must be able to distinguish the specific features of an experience which make him say of it that it is genuine" (pp 117-18). So we are back again to the denial that there can be any cognitive experience that speaks for itself. I have said that all awareness, *as such,* is genuine. How, McPherson is asking, can you distinguish awareness *as such* from something else? My answer is that we can in fact recognise the difference between jumping to a conclusion and registering a fact. The alternative, as I have argued at length, is total scepticism.

The relations between reason and experience will be further explored by an examination of Mr James Richmond's treatment of the topic in his recent book *Theology and Metaphysics* (S.C.M.).

(ii) *James Richmond*

When he speaks of "the logical difficulties in the way of defining *self-authenticating*" (p 18), Richmond seems to disapprove of the sort of appeal to experience which in the end, I hold, we have to make. But he does, eventually, make this appeal himself. It will be worth while to note the stages through which his discussion moves. It begins with an illuminating account of the effects upon German thinking of Kant and Luther with the admirable purpose of showing the necessity of "natural theology" and of deprecating irrational supernaturalism. Richmond proposes "a tentative and comprehensive definition of natural theology: natural theology is the rational construction of a vision of the world as a whole, penetrating beyond the world of appearances to that of ultimate reality, a divine order which is the sole explanation of an experienced world which would otherwise be left obscure, puzzling and unclear" (p 2). And this suggests the performing of logical processes on the basis of sense-presented materials as the natural theologian's business. On the next page Richmond writes: "Within the Augustinian tradition . . . God was regarded as having disclosed himself *generally* to all men through the operation of that divine light which floods all human understanding as such, an operation which is most apparent in the making of aesthetic and moral judgments. God was thus conceived as knowable through his effects; through the operation of that divine light of which God is the sole source." The last sentence of this passage may be described as the Thomist interpretation of Augustine. It seems to me to have been established by scholars that for Augustine there is direct contact with God *in* the "divine light"; God is known not just *through* his effects but *in* them. But I cannot go into the historical question here. What I want to point out is that, even on the interpretation accepted by Richmond, Augustine is not seeking for the "explanation of an experienced world which would otherwise be left obscure, puzzling and unclear", for that obviously refers to some form of the "cosmological" argument. He is finding the explanation of certain facts about *himself*. Richmond returns to this topic, as we shall see, but for a long time he seems simply to dismiss it.

There is something else in his first chapter which needs to be noticed. He explains how the influence of Kant led certain German thinkers to *reduce* God to human experience and to affirm "that what lies supposedly *beyond experience* cannot be of concern or interest to genuine theology" (p 16). And certainly we learn truths from Revelation which may be properly described as being "beyond experience". But it is important to realise that when we are dealing with "natural theology" we must speak of a knowledge of God which is a function of our experience although God himself is not confined to our experience. This is the doctrine of knowledge as "union" which Richmond, I dare say, would not accept. I have the impression that (at least in this chapter) he regards metaphysics simply as a rational construction based on the data of sense-experience and that it is supposed to go "beyond experience" in that sense. Metaphysics, in my view, certainly involves rational analysis (both of "natural" and of "revealed" data, as Richmond very properly insists), but underlying metaphysical analysis there is metaphysical experience.

The second chapter tells (very well) the dreary story of British anti-metaphysical empiricism and goes on to discuss the influence of Wittgenstein, by whom Richmond (like most philosophers with his background) is profoundly impressed. He holds that Wittgenstein offers a means of breaking the deadlock which the "gradual narrowing down of experience to *sense-experience*" (p 23) has brought about. Experience, these words suggest, is going to have a new look. Richmond does not base the suggestion upon Wittgenstein's famous remarks about the "inexpressible" and the "mystical" at the end of his *Tractatus Logico-Philosophicus,* although he is disposed to see in them an admission about "the presence of the ineffable" or "God" (p 32). For Wittgenstein does not regard that as the concern of philosophy. Richmond seems to agree with him, and begins his constructive work (in the third chapter) with Wittgenstein's analysis of "seeing as" towards the end of *Philosophical Investigations*: "Wittgenstein gives the example of the 'duck-rabbit', the image which can be seen *as* a rabbit or *as* a duck. He introduces the concept of *aspect*; we might see a thing for some time under a certain *aspect*: then another *aspect* 'dawns' upon us, and we see something quite different" (p 49). Richmond proposes that we should apply this "to the situation where what is contemplated is not some single object or other, but the world taken as a whole, or, more satisfactorily, *one's entire experience of the world taken as a whole*" (pp 50-51). In other words, we may develop our experience by acts of attention as a result of which we may see what before we had not seen. And this resultant *seeing,* although it is based on facts which are supposed to be available to everyone, is clearly a fresh *cognitive experience.* Is Richmond changing his ground?

He could point out that the "rational construction" of which he spoke earlier is now being explained as "interpretation", which, as he says (p 50), involves a kind of *thinking.* But how do I know that the fresh pattern which I have now come to see is really there, waiting to be seen, and that I have not "put it in" myself? Is it because others agree with me? It would be highly disconcerting if nobody did, but even so for me the pattern *might* obstinately, ineluctably, remain. Should I not then have the "self-authenticating experience" which Richmond has seemed to rule out?

This topic of "interpretation" leads to that of "theistic evidences" in Richmond's fifth chapter. (In the fourth he has shown how some contemporary philosophers have appealed to "interpretation" and there for the first time we find *moral* evidence adduced.) He now turns to "the areas of experience which are held to be theistically evidential", and we find, to our surprise, that the first "may be conveniently called, for want of a better name, the area or dimension of *religious experience*" (p 93). And he goes on to quote, with apparent approval, from the definition of "experience" given in the *Concise Theological Dictionary* of Rahner and Vorgrimler:

"a form of knowledge which arises from the direct reception of an impression from a reality (internal or external) which lies outside our free control. It is contrasted with that type, or aspect of knowledge in which man is an active agent, subjecting the object to his own viewpoints and methods and to critical investigation. An eminent degree of certainty ("evidence") attaches to experience since that which is experienced irresistibly attests to its own presence." Richmond comments: "We must note the insistence here that experience is a form of *knowledge*: what is experienced in this area is not quite so vague and undifferentiated that it escapes conceptualisation and description altogether . . . religious experience is *cognitive*." After all, then, it looks as though Richmond and I were in fundamental agreement about the validity of our basic experience. And he makes a further illuminating comment: "By the use of the words 'irresistibly attests its own presence' Rahner does not, I think, wish to commit himself to the heavily criticised concept of 'self-authentication' as that concept is sometimes dubiously used: rather, by using these words (and by the significant use of '*direct* reception') he is trying quite rightly to emphasise that the religious subject does not make an *inference from* the existence of a certain collection of inner data . . . he claims to experience a reality directly. . . ." This is eminently satisfactory, and I take it that the concept of "self-authentication" is here considered objectionable only in so far as it is used to refer to an alleged supernatural experience which is in no way related to a natural (describable) experience, something which cannot be "pointed to". If this "area" is indeed acknowledged to be "theistically evidential", "rational construction" and "interpretation" will have only a subsidiary or preliminary importance. The reason why the believer believes is that he *sees* something. That is what I mean by a "self-authenticating" experience.

I cannot forbear to mention the impressive passage in which Richmond goes on to show how the effects of the believer's experience can raise the religious question for the unbeliever; indeed, the whole of this chapter is urgently required reading. It is not, however, desirable, I think, to make a sharp distinction between the moral evidence, the second area described, and the first. "Religious experience" must surely be the demand and the attraction of the Good. Nor would I regard the third area, occupied by "existentialist" phenomenology, as properly distinct from the other two, at any rate in regard to Gabriel Marcel. The other areas are "history" (not confined to what is called "salvation history") and "nature", which proves to mean the cosmological and teleological arguments. Contemplation of these areas, Richmond says in effect, can lead one to the conclusion that God is at work in the world, even though no arguments can be produced in logically coercive form. All this is again eminently satisfactory, and I would only add that if in fact one *reaches* the conclusion it must be that God has been *apprehended in* his activity. It is, I think, our incipient awareness of his activity that leads us to ask questions about the world in the first place—metaphysical questions, not just questions about how the world works so that we know how to deal with it. It is God who is questioning us.

The five areas of experience just mentioned were designed to sketch out a map by which a "metaphysical cartographer" might take his bearings. At the beginning of the sixth and final chapter Richmond remarks that in each area the cartographer "has been thrown bafflingly 'beyond' the empirical in his attempt to explain" (p 117). It seems to me that he has done better than that or rather that he has had something more definite done to him. The question is now raised whether the map can be offered to all and sundry. How does it indicate the presence of God? The suggestion that the unbeliever may be asked in the first place to regard "God" as the possible answer to his "intellectual dissatisfactions" (p 119) seems to me of limited usefulness. The technique of "connecting up" the "contingency" found in one area with that found in others (p 120) would seem more promising if the areas themselves became less distinct from one another. The plan here is only to link them, preserving their distinction (p 121). And "God", it is suggested, means the ultimate integrator (p 127). At this point the sceptic is expected to say that he has no justification for making the "desperately unprecedented and unique move" beyond the observable. Can he be offered the "human self or soul" as an *"analogy"*, a "clue", to God (pp 128-9). And we are now (at last) invited to realise that our own *"inner experience of what is involved in thinking and living"* shows that we are ourselves in some way *"outside* the spatio-temporal world"* (pp 130-133). We are back to Augustine.

The last pages of the book make clear that the only significant difference between Richmond's position and mine, so far as presenting evidence for God is concerned, is that he thinks it necessary as a rule to begin with a rather complicated manipulation of "theoretical linking concepts" (p 149); in a discussion with agnostics (and I grant that it may sometimes be necessary), whereas I should as a rule point directly to whatever there may be in their experience which may most readily declare itself to them for what it really is, God's working in them. It has its various aspects (intellectual, moral, aesthetic) but it is always essentially the same. Richmond has taken us on a tortuous but highly profitable journey, and the upshot seems to me clear : we may be led to the experience of God through the use of reason in analysing, linking things up and so forth, but our experience does not *depend* on our reason : it stands on its own feet.

(iii) *Professor E. L. Mascall*

The Gifford Lectures delivered by Professor Mascall in Edinburgh recently, published as *The Openness of Being—Natural Theology Today* (Darton, Longman and Todd), show a point of view which in an important respect is different from mine although not directly opposed to it. We have a great deal in common, and I wish to express my indebtedness to him on many counts. What the difference amounts to is that Mascall regards all appeals to the moral evidence for God as exposed to hazards which he wishes to avoid and therefore confines himself to insisting upon the discovery of "radical contingency uncontaminated by other factors which intrude themselves when I reflect on my own self" (p 15). His approach, in other words, is "cosmological". In the course of some kind remarks about my *Absolute Value* he describes its "argument" as "cosmological with a moral slant rather than as a typical example of the moral argument" in that it appeals to "moral value as a datum apprehended by us in the concrete moral world" (p 8). I gratefully accept that last formulation, but I think that "cosmological" is more naturally understood as referring to the world *outside* (Mascall's "extra-mental being") than to the "concrete moral world", which must here refer primarily to self-knowledge. Behind this, as Mascall has pointed out, there is a certain difference between the accounts which we give of the fundamental human experience. That, for me, is knowledge of self and knowledge of the world outside indissolubly united from the start. Mascall holds that knowledge of the world outside, normally at least, comes first.

It is clear that he does not wish to associate himself with "Christian existentialists" who appeal to *Angst*. But he also mentions, by way of contrasting his own view with it, that of Austin Farrer for whom "my own soul is, not the *only* place, but certainly the *easiest* place in which I can recognise the creative activity of God" (p 15). I am disposed to think that it is the *original* place where this recognition occurs : we know God not just as our Cause but as our End. And there is nothing "existentialist" in the sense of anti-intellectualist about this proposal. Mascall has declared a general policy, in reporting on the present state of natural theology, of leaving aside those writers who regard our awareness of God as bound up with our awareness of themselves. He does, however, quote from Aimé Forest's contribution to *The Many-Faced Argument* (edited by Hick and McGill) : "The ontological argument is the discovery of the absolute; it is necessary to affirm its existence because of the discovery that a presence cannot be reduced to the objectivity of ideas" (p 47). And he goes on to refer to "this very impressive and deeply devout movement of thought". Can there be any awareness of God (of a more than transient kind) which is not "devout"? He also refers to Karl Rahner's view that there is an " 'unthematic' awareness by the mind of itself in every cognitive act" and "of God . . . only as the *principle* of our knowledge" (p 72), and he refers to Coreth, who adopts a similar approach. Nor does he raise any objection, when he quotes from these writers, to their emphasis on self-awareness. It is plain that they are not referring to peculiar emotional states.

There is, I suggest, a certain unwillingness on Mascall's part to accept without reserve the conclusion that the awareness of God is not produced, *effectuated,* by logical argument. He agrees with Rahner and other transcendentalists that "if only we look at finite creatures in the right way we shall see them as created and upheld by that transcendent cause to which we give the name 'God' " (pp 81-2) and with Lonergan that Saint Thomas's Five Ways are "persuasive discourse intended to help us to grasp the fundamental dependence of finite being on infinite being as their ground" (p 89). But he writes later that "the sheer contingency of the objects of our experience demands explanation" (p 120), and when he goes on to speak of the "solid rational grounds" for theism (p 122) he seems to suggest that after all a *logical* move is the *operative* factor in the discovery of God. Still more significantly, he himself raises the question whether "the passage from the recognition of contingent being to the affirmation of necessary being" should be described as an "argument" and says that it depends on just what you mean by "argument" (p 110). Here it is as if he were seeking a half-way house between an "argument" and an apprehension. What happens, I should say, when the move to the apprehension of God is made, is that what was only implicit becomes explicit (and to say this to make a "rational analysis" of the business); God makes himself known to us if we *attend* ("if we only look at creatures in the right way . . ."). *Attention*, I have maintained, is a moral affair *par excellence*. God does indeed "explain" the world : but the reason why we discover him is that he is there to be discovered. It seems to be, in part, Mascall's hesitancy over this matter which accounts for his attitude to the moral evidence.

He continues, however, to espouse the Augustinian thesis of *contuitio*, the apprehension of God *in* the world (his explicit espousal of it some years ago was, to my mind, the most important event in the recent history of the philosophy of religion); and he continues to maintain his neutrality in regard to the question of the *place* where *contuitio* occurs. He writes : "Now I do not wish to quarrel with the stress which, for their own purposes, both Farrer and [Professor H. P.] Owen place upon the human self as the datum for theistic argumentation," and he speaks of Owen's "extremely impressive argument", adding, however, at once : "I prefer to start from beings that we know more objectively and at the same time less intimately than we know ourselves" on the ground that there is then "no danger of confusion with those psychological states of insecurity and anxiety to which existentialists attribute direct ontological status" (pp 108-110). On the face of it, then, that is the only reason for maintaining neutrality. I take it that he is questioning the "existentialist" claim on the ground that the "psychological states" which he mentions could be the basis only for an argument of an unsatisfactory kind to the presence of God. It was worth while to return to his justified suspicion of such a claim, for the difference between that sort of claim and my own may be now made more precise. I am not saying that we first take cognisance of our human condition in a state of tension and then go on somehow to discover God's action upon us; I am proposing that we discover his activity, his summons, *in* that tension. And the "tension" is no extraordinary condition but the character of that awareness of the general moral demand which can be adverted to without special emotional excitement and at all times. We do not first look into ourselves and then (as a subsequent development) start looking for God. When we *attend*, we are looking at ourselves and God together. We are being truly "objective", because they *are* together, and it would be better to speak of looking through ourselves than to speak of looking *into* ourselves. We look out at what is there. This is, to my mind, what *contuitio* ought to mean, and it is regularly on the basis of this, I think, that we recognise God's activity in the world at large.

Mascall points to the danger of making mistakes about knowledge of the self. We *can*, as I have said, make mistakes about anything if we do not guard against them. I am not sure whether he would agree with me that whether we are talking about the moral claim or about the "contingency" of the world outside it is the character of our experience as objective on which we have to satisfy ourselves. Admittedly when we are considering the world outside we can check our results by those of other people in a way which is impossible when we are considering the moral demand. But I have tried to show that the *guarantee* of objectivity must always be itself "subjective" in the sense that we must always fall back in the end on the validity of our own experience. Mascall does mention (neutrally) this insistence of mine on the absolute certainty of human awareness simply as such in his remarks about *Absolute Value*; but he does not seem to feel it necessary himself to contest the assertion so frequently accepted by natural theologians that we can never be sure of avoiding mistakes, although in his Appendix on Boyce Gibson's book, which I discuss in the next chapter, he had a very obvious opportunity of doing so. He recognises that I insist on absolute certainty for the particular reason that all recognition of *truth* is itself, in my view, a recognition of God. And this is the place to emphasise that this recognition is no abstract consideration but, to adapt the formula which I have gratefully accepted from Mascall, the recognition of intellectual value as a datum apprehended in the concrete, the recognition that this particular act of intelligence, bearing upon this particular object, has come up against the ground of being as against a solid rock. In appealing to the nature of knowledge one is necessarily referring at the same time to the character of the objects known. And this character, for me, is that of "groundedness" rather than that of "contingency", when we are concerned simply with objects in the world outside us. I do not deny the possibility that the discovery of "groundedness" may be the discovery of God for the first time; but I doubt whether this is normally the way in which that discovery is first made. Even so it must be followed by the recognition that the truth *ought* to be known.

The difference between Mascall's approach and mine has, I believe, a considerable importance for practical purposes. It seems to me that what I refer to as the fact of moral obligation is in point of fact the most "objective" thing there is for many people. When it comes to the crunch, and everything solid seems to be collapsing into the void of relativism, it is the demand of value (which may be, to repeat, the value of *truth*) which prevents their giving up the attempt to make sense of themselves and of the world in which they live. If, as I think, they can be legitimately encouraged to *dwell* on this demand in the hope of clearing their minds, it is obviously important that they should be so encouraged. When Mascall tells them that beings must either explain themselves or have some explanation beyond themselves (p 110), such people may find it extremely difficult or even impossible to satisfy themselves that *this* question of explanation need arise at all. Certainly some things act on other things in our world, and you can explain what happens in terms of these activities. But the system of the universe is not itself seen to *happen* unless we are going to leave out the stage of demanding explanations and claim instead that God can be "detected" at work in it. I shall not discuss further what "detection" must mean in this context, for I have now done all I can to indicate it. It is this *contuitio* which Mascall, I believe, is really concerned to put before us as all-important, despite the talk of rational demands and explanations. But it seems to me that it is quite easy to be in doubt about the detection of God's activity in the external world and to consider whether one's suspicion of it is just an affective state. Mascall seems to think that this difficulty attaches especially, if not exclusively, to the discovery of God's activity exercised upon one's own spiritual powers. But he allows, of course, or rather insists, that people today do find it very difficult "to look at finite creatures in the right way".

Finally I want to mention two passages in which Mascall gives his valuable support to positions which I take up in this book. Criticising the "positivist attitude" he writes : "I do not think that even the later Wittgenstein and his successors have clearly seen that the nature and function of language are not exhausted by a discussion of either its internal logic or the speech-behaviour of people who use it . . . there is a real sense in which meaning is fundamentally mental and is logically prior to language" (pp 20-21).

(He goes on to take a stand against relativism which one might have expected to lead to a discussion of absolute certainty.) In the second of these passages, speaking of the use of analogical terms used with reference to God, he tells us that he has "come to see more clearly that one is already loading the question if one puts it in the form 'How can terms which in their normal and natural application refer to finite beings refer analogically to God?' ". And he goes on : "The primary datum, although many modern empirical philosophers may not be ready to admit this, is that the terms apply *both* to finite beings *and* to God, and the question is how this dual application can be explained . . . only the notion of a God who is related to the world—and who is related to it in a very particular way—can make the fact of this dual applicability of terms intelligible" (pp 33-34). In other words, I think we must conclude, *contuitio* reveals God as the source and infinite exemplar of the values which we find in created things.

CHAPTER NINE MODERN THINKERS AND CERTAINTY

(i) *Ludwig Wittgenstein*

The obvious text to concentrate on is Ludwig Wittgenstein's *On Certainty* (edited by G. E. M. Anscombe and G. H. von Wright, and translated by Denis Paul and G. E. M. Anscombe, Blackwell, 1969), a collection of notes on which he was engaged during the last eighteen months of his life. I shall refer to the notes by their numbers. From the beginning the notion of a self-guaranteeing awareness is excluded. For example, we read : "It needs to be *shown* that no mistake was possible. Giving the assurance 'I know' doesn't suffice. For it is after all only an assurance that I can't be making a mistake, and it needs to be *objectively* established that I am not making a mistake about *that*" (15). Clearly my claim to a certainty is not conclusive proof *for somebody else* that what I say is true. From his point of view there must remain the possibility that I am mistaken. But if I am indeed *aware* of my own body and of a body not my own impinging on mine there can be no question of *my* requiring further proof of it. Unless this is accepted, I have argued, we condemn ourselves to a complete and self-refuting scepticism. For we shall be unable to give any sense to the notion of *truth,* yet we shall be compelled all the same to operate with it. This will become clearer as we proceed.

In 21 Wittgenstein considers the view that a statement beginning with "I know" can't be a mistake. His comment is that "if that *is* so, then there can be an inference from such an utterance to the truth of an assertion". And in 30 he remarks : "One does not infer how things are from one's own certainty", to which is added : "Certainty is *as it were* a tone of voice in which one declares how things are, but one does not infer from the tone of voice that one is justified." These statements might at first seem to indicate that Wittgenstein is rejecting the *need* for inference as I do. But that he is not in agreement is clear from, for example, 38 : "Knowledge in mathematics : Here one has to keep on reminding oneself of the unimportance of the 'inner process' or 'state' and ask 'Why should it be important? What does it matter to me?' What is interesting is how we *use* mathematical propositions." I reject the need for inference because the mental "process", which is not merely "inner" but my *union* with an *object,* is itself my guarantee. Wittgenstein is saying that there is no guarantee and that it is wrongheaded to require one. Doubt is senseless in certain circumstances, he will tell us, for in these the language-game forbids the expression of doubt. The ultimate appeal is not to *truth* but to how things *work*. So 39 reads : *"This* is how calculation is done, in such circumstances a calculation is *treated* as absolutely reliable, as certainly correct"; whereas "I know that I am in pain" is "wrong" (41) because there is no use for it in the language-game.

The opposition to the point of view which I have been putting forward is very clear in 47 : "Calculating is *this*. What we learnt at school, for example. Forget this transcendent certainty, which is connected with your concept of spirit." Indeed it is difficult to see how any "concept of spirit" is compatible with the conclusion to which Wittgenstein is now moving. He does not reach it explicitly for some time. It emerges clearly enough in 94, where "my picture of the world" is said to be "the inherited background against which I distinguish between true and false". So there can be no question about the truth and falsity of the background, for truth is *relative* to it. There is no absolute truth, for "the same proposition may get treated at one time as something to test by experience, at another as a rule for testing" (98). The inherited language-game changes, and truth changes with it. We are forbidden, apparently, to ask : is *that theory* true? But, I contend, we must be allowed to ask the question. It does mean something.

In 108 Wittgenstein asks himself whether there is any "objective truth". But his reply is, as before, that we can only speak of things "within our system" and that if anyone makes a claim which is inconsistent with it we "should feel ourselves intellectually very distant" from him. And in 135 we have the suggestion that the problem of induction (why do we believe that "what has always happened will happen again"?) is abolished by appealing to a *"natural law* which our inferring apparently follows". Since the alleged problem has no effect upon the conduct of our lives it is "not an item in our considerations". Again we are faced with a pragmatist conclusion.

It begins to appear that Wittgenstein is interested, in a discussion about knowledge, only with what can be discovered by an investigation conducted on scientific lines. Knowledge as actual experience and so as certainty is not considered. So certainty becomes what "stands fast" in the system of our thought because that system happens to be what it is. It could be a different one. "Moore does not *know* what he asserts he knows, but it stands fast for him . . ." (151). Wittgenstein harps on the theme that we gain knowledge by *learning*, not, that is to say, by a mental contact with reality.

"The difficulty", he writes, "is to realise the groundlessness of our believing" . . . (166). In other words, we must just go on living and stop asking questions. But this is a special form of pragmatism. It is not simply that propositions "stand fast" because it pays us to accept them. It is that, if we play the language-game, which derives from a certain form of life, we *must* accept them. "Giving grounds, however, justifying the evidence, comes to an end;—but the end is not certain propositions striking us as immediately true, i.e. it is not a kind of *seeing* on our part; it is our *acting*, which lies at the bottom of the language-game" (204). It is plain to me that there *is* a kind of seeing on our part, but one which is, fundamentally, not of propositions but of things. Wittgenstein, however, after asking what use we have for a statement beginning "I *know*", lays it down again that "it is not a question of mental processes or mental states" (230). And in 245 he says : "There is no subjective sureness that I know something. The certainty is subjective, but not the knowledge." I should say that certain knowledge or knowledge in the strong sense is subjective in so far as it is ours but objective in the sense that it puts us in touch with what is not ourselves. It is the cognitive character of our basic experience which is being overlooked by Wittgenstein.

The rejection of absolute truth leads, naturally, to some very curious conclusions. For example, we find in 262 : "I can imagine a man who had grown up in quite special circumstances and had been taught that the world came into being fifty years ago, and therefore believes this. We might instruct him : the earth has long . . . etc.—We should be trying to give him our picture of the world." And the remark is added : "This would happen through a kind of *persuasion*." This means, I take it, that we should be persuading him to adopt our language-game or form of life. We should be inviting him to accept it as convenient for him, presumably. Anyone who follows Wittgenstein in this matter must realise what is involved in this abandonment of the commonsense notion of *objective fact*. 267 reads : "I don't merely have the visual impression of a tree : I know that it is a tree." Wittgenstein puts the sentences in inverted commas. I accept what they say, on the ground that I make intellectual contact with an object which I call a tree *in* my visual impression of it. In 270 the "grounds" of a certainty are said to make it "objective". But this means that there are "countless general empirical propositions that *count as* certain for us" (273—my italics) and that "Experience can be said to teach us these propositions" (274), but that "If experience is the ground of our certainty, then naturally it is past experience" (275). In other words, it is our *inheritance* which provides objective (public) certainty. Is there no certainty in the private experience of here and now? Our convictions about the earth's antiquity obviously do depend on our past experience and that of others. So does our use of language. But our present *awareness* lies behind what we say.

I am not sure how to take 286, where Wittgenstein says "We all believe that it isn't possible to go to the moon; but there might be people who believe that it is possible . . . If we compare our system of knowledge with theirs, then theirs is evidently the poorer one by far." "We all" means, apparently "a community which is bound together by science and education" (298). I am not sure on what grounds another system of knowledge is being compared with ours to its disadvantage. But I take it that a relatively incomplete system is being compared with a relatively complete one within the same language-game. For different language-games would be, presumably, *just* different. They are the systems within which discriminations are made. It would seem that we cannot discriminate between *them*. In 338 Wittgenstein considers another class of persons as extraordinary, those "who say that it is merely extremely probable that water over a fire will boil and not freeze" (instead of being "quite certain" of it). He asks : "What difference does it make in their lives? Isn't it just that they talk rather more about certain things than the rest of us?" This I find very hard to interpret. I can only suppose that these people are thought to be living a form of life which is a variant of the normal form with the result that they have certain extraordinary interests. They are thus modifying the language-game in their use of it. They are succeeding in disregarding what Wittgenstein called in 135 a *"natural law* which our inferring apparently follows". It seems to me that they are facing a real problem which presents itself to our minds. The "uniformity of nature" is only a postulate, and we rightly seek for its ground in *reality*. If we do not attach any meaning to *reality* here, the strangest paradoxes face us.

In 348 Wittgenstein says that "the words 'I am here' have a meaning only in certain contexts . . . not because they are elsewhere superfluous, but because their meaning is not *determined* by the situation, yet stands in need of such determination." Clearly there is a sense in which these words can be said to have a different meaning in different circumstances. But it seems plain to me that there is also a sense in which they have a meaning (the *same* meaning) in all circumstances. If that is being denied, as apparently it is, this sort of pragmatism leads again to paradox.

It must be recognised that Wittgenstein is only feeling his way in all this. When, after speaking of a *"comfortable* certainty", he says "I would like to regard this certainty, not as something akin to hastiness or superficiality, but as a form of life", he adds in brackets that this "is very badly expressed and probably badly thought" (357-8). But the point is that the rejection of certainty as cognitive experience *must* lead to an anti-intellectualism. So in 359 we read : "But that means I want to conceive it [the certainty] as something that lies beyond being justified or unjustified, as it were, as something animal." This leads to the suggestion that knowledge is "related to a decision" (362), and we read in 368 : "If someone says that he will recognise no experience as proof of the opposite, that is after all a *decision*. It is possible that he will act against it." As an account of certainty I find this unintelligible. If Wittgenstein thought that there should be no question at this point of intelligibility, then I should say that he had given up philosophy. In my view, if you are certain of anything (but you can be certain only on the basis of actual experience—although this could include experience of a reliable authority *as* reliable), you are certain that no subsequent experience *can* contradict it. *Seeing* a logical connection is, of course, an experience no less and no more than seeing a material object.

Wittgenstein's final appeal may be to something "animal", something which is not intelligible, but his concern with philosophy is a concern with logic. We must "make sense" of things even if this means that we come up eventually against brute fact which stops the process. If that interpretation of him is right, 390 is particularly interesting : "All that is important is that it makes sense to say that one knows such a thing; and consequently the assurance that one does know it can't accomplish anything here" (these notes of Wittgenstein's were provoked by G. E. Moore's famous claim to know that he had two hands). He has said in 389 : "A personal experience simply has no interest for us here." 390 gives the reason for this—"making sense" means fitting something in with the logic of the language-game. But there is another way of "making sense". When I have asked whether one can make sense of certain statements about God, I have been asking whether such statements are based on a genuine experience of God. What *makes* sense is the certainty of experience itself. It is always contact with sense at its source, that is, with God. You cannot make *sense of* certainty. It *is* sense. Wittgenstein is thus turning our situation inside out. What we cannot make sense of is not, as he seems to be saying, brute fact but intelligibility itself. There is no proof of certainty not, as he seems to think, because it brings us up against a final darkness but because it is itself the light in which we see everything. In that case it is the turning away from experience to logic which is the fundamental error. Moore was right. He is asking us whether we do not share his *experience*. Thinking logically, moreover, is our *experience* of following the connections which are really *there*.

403 is perhaps the most explicit statement of the view to which Wittgenstein's thoughts regularly recur : "To say of man, in Moore's sense, that he *knows* something; that what he says is therefore unconditionally the truth, seems wrong to me.—It is truth only inasmuch as it is an unmoving foundation of his language-games." And in 422 he admits that he is "trying to say something that sounds like pragmatism". Since he has spoken in 411 of the assumption that the earth has existed for many years past as forming "the basis of action, and therefore, naturally, of thought" and quoted Goethe's "In the beginning was the deed" in 402, it is at any rate clear that he does not give the primacy to cognition. But he is still hesitant : "Do I want to say, then, that certainty resides in the nature of the language-game?" (457). For he has to face the question : how is doubt introduced into the language-game? How can we escape its constraints? For obviously we do. I do not find that we are given any answer to the question. 475, however, shows the bias of Wittgenstein's thought : "I want to regard man here . . . as a primitive being to which one grants instincts but not ratiocination . . . Language did not emerge from some kind of ratiocination.' Presumably, then, it arises as a form of action in obedience to a blind will for survival or development. Or is it itself the ultimate mystery? Wittgenstein seems now to be set on rejecting our specifically human powers : "experience", for him, is not itself cognitive. In 477 he asks why we should have to *know* "that the objects whose name one teaches a child . . . exist", suggesting that it is enough that "experience doesn't later show" that they do not, and adding "why should the language-game rest on some kind of knowledge?" And in 478, after asking whether a child knows that milk exists, he asks : "Does a cat know that a mouse exists?"

Naturally, then, he concludes: "It is as if 'I know' did not tolerate a metaphysical emphasis" (482).

No one can avoid metaphysics in the end. Some sort of world-picture is going to emerge, and Wittgenstein's emerges more and more. In 503 he considers one's holding to a statement "I know that that's a tree" when everybody and everything is against it—and asks: "what *good* would it do me to stick to my 'I know'?" This suggests that sticking to one's statement ought to be a function of some grand *design* in which one co-operates. And in 505 there is apparently mention of such a design: "It is always by favour of Nature that one knows something." The attempt to avoid metaphysics leads to the adoption in practice of a vague metaphysics with possibly sinister implications. Falling back on the instinctual level, for instance, as an ultimate court of appeal is obviously dangerous. 509 reads: "I really want to say that a language-game is only possible if one trusts something." If one cannot trust one's own experience, if one does not know *the truth*, then one does have to rely on "Nature". And that this is a blind sort of reliance seems pointed to in 559: "You must bear in mind that the language-game is so to say something unpredictable. I mean: it is not based on grounds. It is not reasonable (or unreasonable)." And Wittgenstein adds: "It is there—like our life." There are over a hundred entries after that, but they get us no further. I pick out one of them to indicate the relativism which Wittgenstein is now definitely proposing (he is considering people who might consult an oracle instead of a physicist). "Is it wrong for them to consult an oracle and be guided by it?—If we call this 'wrong' aren't we using our language-game as a base from which to *combat* theirs?" (609).

(ii)   *Ilham Dilman*

Anyone who disagrees with Wittgenstein is likely to be told by his disciples that he has misunderstood him. So it was satisfactory to discover that Mr Ilham Dilman in a review-article of *On Certainty* (in *Philosophy* for April 1971) gives the same sort of account of it, though going into more detail, as I do—but with no hint of disagreement with Wittgenstein. Indeed he tells us that these notes "constitute a first-rate contribution to epistemology and logic" and that Wittgenstein has made "new progress" here, that is, he has improved on his former writings on the subject, not going back on them but going further in the direction already taken by them. Dilman quotes a good many of the entries which I have selected as showing the conclusions to which Wittgenstein comes, and there is no point at which his glosses on them differ significantly from mine, *except* that he regards Wittgenstein's conclusions as acceptable and I do not. He does not mention the hesitancies to which I have drawn attention, regarding them presumably as incidental or perhaps as part of a "dialectical" method.

It will be useful in connection with this review-article to return to the question to which I referred just now about the way in which, according to Wittgenstein, there can be a *combat* between the players of different language-games. Dilman quotes Wittgenstein's reference to a possible opposition between Catholics who say that the consecrated wine in the Mass is blood and Moore who may say "I know that this wine is not blood" (239). He comments: "Wittgenstein means that the Catholics would be unmoved . . . There is no common system between what Catholics hold and what Moore might maintain here for these to contradict each other: 'Would you say they believe the opposite?' Compare Wittgenstein's discussion of this whole question in *Lectures on Religious Belief*. Also connect with what he says in his 'Lectures on Ethics' about judgements of absolute value and how they are an expression of an attitude to the world as a whole, an expression of a way of looking at life and of meeting its problems." Wittgenstein's example is not a happy one, for it is not Catholic doctrine that the wine undergoes a chemical change; what is asserted is that it becomes the vehicle for the activity of the risen Christ, a statement which will seem unfounded for the unbeliever. Certainly it cannot be disproved. But it is either true or untrue. A believer may be said to play a special language-game in so far as he uses words as "pointers" to God and will not be understood by those who have no apprehension of God. But he is not appealing to a special kind of *truth*. Wittgenstein speaks of *persuading* an unbeliever, but he does not understand in what this persuading consists. It is a persuading to open the mind for a fresh discovery. But what is chiefly important here is that, on Dilman's showing, judgements of absolute value and judgements about religion are, for Wittgenstein, expressions of "an attitude towards the world" or of "a way of looking at life and of meeting its problems". They are not expressions of absolute *truth,* for there is nothing which deserves that description. People who seek support for religion from Wittgenstein must recognise that they are taking up with a philosophy which must be characterised as anti-intellectualist. They are in danger of exchanging faith for fideism.

Dilman writes : "If Wittgenstein stressed the importance of acquiring skills and habits in the learning of language he certainly never confined it to this. If there is something in language that we begin to learn by rote, almost like an animal, there is much in connection with speaking, thinking and expressing ourselves that goes beyond what can be learnt in this way. Consider the development of judgement, imagination and talent in the use of language, for instance, in literature, or in human relationships, or in scientific research. If Wittgenstein emphasised the importance of rules in connection with the use of words that is because he wanted to bring into prominence the way in which the distinction between using words correctly and incorrectly underlies the possibility of using them to say something." All this sounds reasonable enough and might suggest that I have, after all, misunderstood Wittgenstein. But how is the distinction just mentioned itself *grasped*? Do we never really *grasp* anything? The ultimate question is rejected. If we do not experientally *know* what we are doing in the development of judgement, imagination and the rest of it, then we can have no "world-picture" at all (we merely "live") or rather, as I have suggested, we unwittingly take up with one. At the end of his article Dilman writes : "It makes no sense to find fault with a language-game as a whole. If this can be made clear much will have been done towards meeting philosophical scepticism. To meet it means coming to a better understanding of what we are concerned to understand in philosophy. It does not make anything secure, or more secure, for those carrying on with the various activities in their life, those engaged in various forms of research." I do not understand how philosophical scepticism is met if nothing is secure—except that certain philosophers have found something definite to do : logic, the playing of a language-game.

(iii) *A. Boyce Gibson*

The rejection of absolute certainty has been further encouraged by Wittgenstein, but it was a feature of British and American empiricism long before his time. I must know give some fresh examples of the doctrine against which I have been protesting for so many years. First I shall take Professor A. Boyce Gibson's recent book *Theism and Empiricism* (S.C.M. Press) which illustrates the time-honoured method of rejection, consisting in the end simply in the contention that, since we are sometimes *convinced* about something and prove to be wrong, therefore we can never be really certain. My answer, to repeat, is simply that, although if we are not careful we *can* always jump to conclusions, it is nevertheless possible for us to register our experience without doing this. It is possible, for example, as I have said, to be aware that one sees a logical connection and that one is as a matter of fact *not* wrong about this. Boyce Gibson takes the popular view for granted and writes : "The appeal to experience can never be conclusive . . ." (p 24), a remark which he repeats in various forms on a good many occasions. This leads him (or at any rate helps to lead him) to the conclusion that religious assurance "does not rest on intellectual certainty" (p 13) and does not need to do so; our awareness of God leaves us uncertain, but "the commitment of faith" turns it into a state of mind which is indeed sometimes described as certainty but more often as one of confidence not exempt from doubt (that I take to be Boyce Gibson's considered view). It will be remembered that I have allowed for the coexistence of an undeveloped faith and doubt but maintained that faith does *of its nature* convey certainty.

But what Boyce Gibson says of "religious experience" goes further at one point. He holds in general that it can never settle anything for us, but he does recognise that without it the philosophy of religion can never get off the ground, and in the passage in question, speaking of the individual's "report" of his "religious knowledge", he writes : "We know that it is not the last word, but we are absolutely sure of it as far as it goes" (p 52). If this means that our knowledge, though limited, can be absolutely true, then we are at this point in apparent agreement. But it is, I fear, only an apparent agreement in any case in so far as this "religious experience" depends upon the "commitment of faith", which, as we have seen, does not require "intellectual certainty". We do not *see* the truth, but somehow or other it can be bestowed upon us as a result of our act of *trust,* our taking a plunge. There is certainly a strong pragmatist or voluntarist strain running through this book which seems to derive largely from Kant. But it seems to me that Boyce Gibson sometimes comes within hailing distance of the view that we must accept God's summons before our knowledge of him can be supernatural and in principle *secure*. We must be definitively aware of this summons, I have maintained, before we can accept it and in so doing gain the fresh evidence of *faith*. But until we have done so this awareness is at risk in that we can banish it from consciousness more readily than we can banish faith. And this "natural knowledge" of God, as I have called it, is thus not discoverable in practice apart from the supernatural knowledge of faith, for, if the summons is rejected, it goes underground, for the time being at least. Grace is always "on offer", but if we reject it we become deaf to the summons.

Boyce Gibson's acceptance of the "uncertainty principle" is particularly remarkable because he is advocating an "empirical metaphysics" (in that, to my mind, lies the considerable importance of his book). He has no use for the cutting-off of religion from the rest of our experience. He is not at all inclined to reduce human experience to something quite different. He makes the necessary criticism of Kant : "though he understood that the science of his time was a *necessary* knowledge of empirical phenomena, he did not similarly admit that there might be an *empirical* knowledge of things in themselves" (p 21). On the relation between "ought" and "is" he remarks, in the same genuinely empirical spirit : "Religion carries to a higher point an association which belongs to experience from the very beginning" (p 31). And on "the attempt to recover the cause from the effect" he writes : "if the effect does not in some sense *overlap* with the cause, no such recovery is possible. What is called an effect is a presence, not merely a proxy or a signpost" (pp 63-4). All this should be leading him to the claim that a cognitive experience of God is available for man. But, since he believes (on the authority, it would seem, of the modern dogma) that there can be no *certainty* in experience itself, he is led to substitute an appeal to action instead at the critical points in his discussion, and even then, as we have seen, he is usually unwilling to speak of "certainty" without qualification—naturally, because if certainty is not a matter of cognitive experience an attempt to account for it in other terms will meet with insuperable difficulties. "Action" may indeed *lead* to certainty if that means following up a suspicion (the agnostic's prayer). But truth is discovered in that *experience* which is our specific, fundamental characteristic.

I have spoken of a "genuinely empirical spirit". It seems to me very strange that those who call themselves "empiricists" should have adopted the principle that we can never rely absolutely on our experience. It seems so obvious that there can be no test of experience (because we should then need to test the test itself) and that we must therefore choose between accepting our experience simply as a matter of practical necessity or accepting it as what it presents itself to us as being, when we attend to and submit to it, a contact with reality and its source. If we are not going to give up philosophy for the practical necessity of keeping alive and "developing", the only alternative to accepting our experience as it presents itself to us seems the betaking ourselves to the study of language, the logic of the language-game, as the philosophers of the generation junior to Boyce Gibson's have commonly done (his book has met, of course, with the criticism that his whole point of view is out of date). And an examination of Wittgenstein's conclusions seems to have shown that this study of language is itself only a function of a language-game or a "form of life" in a sense which precludes us from saying that it is either a true form or a false one. Of course one cannot do philosophy *without* a study of language, and contemporary philosophers have shown this most usefully. But logic is not an end in itself—especially when logicians can never be certain whether they are are really seeing a logical connection or not. All this paragraph has been repetition, and I must again repeat that seeing such a connection is itself an experience.

(iv) *Keith Ward*

There are clear signs that a reaction against linguistic philosophy is under way, but the "uncertainty principle" is still taken for granted on all sides. We shall see it in operation again if I now turn to certain passages in another recent book which contains much of great value, especially on the "objectivism" of ethics and on the moral evidence for God, Mr Keith Ward's *Ethics and Christianity* (Allen and Unwin). But first I must give some indication of his position in regard to Christian *faith*. "The notion of 'revelation'," he writes, "is closely allied to the notions of 'authority' and 'experience'. The moral authority is one who has a greater and deeper experience of that which his followers experience in some degree; and what he tells them of his own experience becomes 'revelation' for them" (p 163). But he deprecates the notion that " 'revelation' should be regarded as 'self-disclosure' of God's nature directly to men . . .", for "it is probable that very few persons ever come near to apprehension of the truth of God's nature (the nature of the *Good, qua* ground of ethical claims) in this way . . . On the other hand, the notion of 'revelation' cannot be entirely dissociated from that of 'experience', for otherwise it would be difficult to see on what grounds anything could be accepted as revealed. It seems that what is required is the notion of an 'authoritative experient' whose word other men trust as expressing a level of insight to which they cannot attain . . ." (p 164). Such an account of accepting Christ's authority I have regarded as insufficient; faith, in the New Testament, is something more than this. And I should say that there is an awareness of God (a "revelation" in the broad sense of the term) "*qua* ground of ethical claims", although of course commonly in an inarticulate form, in the awareness of absolute obligation, which is not, as Ward seems to hold, something *extraordinary*.

Ward goes on to speak of "a personal experience of an immanent presence of the objective ideal in one" as something which "one must perhaps ultimately fall back on" in the face of naturalistic accounts of our moral experience, but he adds : "I am certainly not saying that commitment to the ideal is to be *founded on* personal experience—as though one could establish the existence of something by the simple claim to have experienced it . . ." (p 165). Here is the "uncertainty principle" at work again. It is true that one may not attain experience of "the ideal" without the help of an authority and without the need for processes of reasoning as a preliminary, but if "commitment to the ideal" is to be intellectually justified must it not be itself *founded on* this experience? In his first chapter, in which he speaks as the devil's advocate, Ward has asked : "Does it not follow then that the Christian who makes a total, unconditional commitment to the truth of his faith does something which is unreasonable?" (p 24). The "commitment to the ideal", he now seems to answer, is in fact *not* total and unconditional. Or would he say that the *tests* of an authority's reliability to which he refers can be wholly convincing? How could they be unless they led us to an experience of the authority such that his reliability could not remain in question, an experience of God revealing? Ward remarks that he claims here to establish only "the notion of authoritative revelation in religion, and to show that it has a moral basis", and that this is "not sufficient to establish the truth or uniqueness of the Christian revelation", for that requires "an examination of the concepts of 'the Fall', 'Atonement' and 'Redemption', which assure the uniqueness of Jesus . . ."

(p 167). What he says later about these concepts does indeed point most valuably to the "uniqueness" of Jesus, but he does not in fact claim that the *truth* of Christianity can be *established* by such an examination.

Ward now proceeds to discuss directly "the thorny problem of the validity of religious experience" (p 168). An experience of *God,* he tells us, cannot be experience of "any object which is not apprehended as total claim" or "any object which does not demand of us both dread and reverence . . ." So far, of course, I agree. But he goes on : "It can be seen that these criteria are established not just on the basis of some supposedly 'self-authenticating' experience . . . but by reflection on the foundation of our moral beliefs, the facts of the human situation in the light of those beliefs, a sympathetic consideration of the claims of those whom we believe to be more ethically perceptive than ourselves and an honest appraisal of our own state of moral development and insight" (pp 169-70). And again I agree that an experience which is not a "self-authenticating" one or, more precisely, an experience which constitutes only a "suspicion" of God, may depend upon the use of such criteria and may require a further use of them if it is to acquire greater validity. But what is essentially required is a persevering *attention* paid to it. And it may then *become* a "self-authenticating" experience. It seems to me simply a prejudice to deny that there can ever be such an experience. All cognitive experience, I have maintained, is as such self-authenticating in that it is a conscious union with an object. It occurs in a context. Its occurrence is *conditioned* by a variety of previous occurrences. But its *meaning* is given to it by its object—by that with which one is in conscious union (in *that* sense alone we must speak of God as an "object"). And this object can be characterised—negatively, as Ward points out. Sometimes the most illuminating way of doing so will be to say that we are in union with the *inexpressible.* Others may or may not recognise what we are talking about in their own experience. But that makes no difference to ours.

Ward, however, follows up the statements last quoted from him with the claim that "it is not just the intrinsic character of an experience which certifies its genuineness as an experience of God; it is also its consonance with a whole system of concepts by means of which we interpret our moral experience, and which do or do not support and corroborate each other as we find them leading us to expectations (about the character of future experience) which are subsequently fulfilled". He does reject the view that "there is no specific characteristic, or inner quality, of the experience itself, over and above that 'read into' it by the interpretative concepts . . ." (p 170), but he appears to think that this characteristic can never be itself discriminated with certainty. For he goes on to consider whether "one could ostensively define God to *oneself*", raising by way of answer the following questions : "But then, how could one convey to others its meaning? Or how could one convey its implications even to oneself?" (p 171). What has to be said about this is that the apprehension of God occurs in a moral context, or, more precisely, that God is apprehended as the Good and our goal. We recognise him as the goal to which we have been obscurely drawn throughout our lives. But it is not until the inexpressible difference between God and his creatures, in other words, the inexpressibility of God, has been itself apprehended that we can speak of an apprehension of *him*. It is contact with him that gives our religious experience its "inner quality", and although this is bound up with our experience as a whole there appears to be no ground at all for denying that it can be self-authenticating in the sense which should now be clear. If it is not already self-authenticating, it can be strengthened ("corroborated") by further relating of it with our experience in general, but it stands (when it does stand) always on its own feet.

That conclusion is sometimes rejected by modern philosophers for one or other of two special reasons (or for both at the same time), which may be conveniently mentioned at this point. One is the supposition that by a "self-authenticating experience" is meant an experience of a highly peculiar kind in that a special "guaranteeing" feature is attached to the experience or that the object of it is found to be possessed of a special feature of "guaranteedness". I have already dealt with this in principle, but something more needs to be said. What ought to be meant by this experience is that one is in the presence of something which is simply given. Now this notion is anathema to many modern philosophers. No doubt there is interpretation involved in all our experience, but (I have maintained) there is always *something* to be interpreted, and it is possible in certain circumstances to discriminate it. The point which I want to emphasise here is that what is simply given and taken as such is a reality (whether or not it is accurately describable) apprehended as such, that is to say, as truly a part of the world's furniture—and by saying "truly", I have argued, we are indicating that it belongs to a system of reality which has a source, a foundation : we are in touch with the foundation. What is given, then, is God's created world *as* created, the world and God *as* creator. It is *God* who is the explanation of "givenness". There is no question of justifying the notion of "givenness" *in order to* justify that of God. The awareness of God explains things to us : it cannot be itself explained (the alternative, I have tried to show, is to give language-games this ultimacy). That awareness may seem "peculiar" to an agnostic. To me it is just what knowledge means. To know is to know the truth. If nothing is given, there is no truth. One either accepts or rejects this position *as a whole*. In the end there is no arguing about it.

The second of the special reasons for rejecting this experience is that the believer is supposed to *require* reasons to support his belief even though his belief may not be thought to rest originally upon them. Until reasons are forthcoming, it is suggested, his belief cannot be recognised by him as a true one. If he is certain, I reply, then there will always in fact be reasons for his belief, some of which will presumably have helped him towards it, in the sense that the state of affairs in the world will be not only compatible with it but in principle explicable by it. For truth cannot contradict truth. But it is a mistake to suppose that such a belief requires to be *checked* by such considerations. What requires to be checked is not certain.

Here I may add (or rather repeat) that I am not decrying a "commitment" to what seems (perhaps overwhelmingly) *probable*, provided that it is recognised for what it is. What is to be deplored is the denial of a doubt in circumstances in which doubt (however slight) must (logically) remain. Ward at one point says that "trust is necessary" and speaks of "a challenge which calls for total commitment", although faith is "not a demonstrable truth" (p 202). What is it then?

In his review of my *Absolute Value* (in *Theology*, June, 1971) Ward revealed himself as far more of a Wittgensteinian than I had supposed. His criticism of the book is that it "tends to give a short answer to philosophical problems by appealing to direct experience". Referring to my claims about our awareness of God, he writes : "The view that one can be aware of so many sophisticated notions needs some defence against the criticisms of Wittgenstein, which have convinced most philosophers in this respect . . . assertion is no substitute for argument." As regards "sophisticated

might perhaps suggest even to a determinist philosopher that a failure to live up to the standards of one's profession may be something more than an eccentricity.

For that is all it can be on a "positivist" showing. If our errant philosopher wants to save himself trouble in this way, a positivist cannot say that he *ought* not to in the sense which still operates, however obscurely, in the minds of ordinary people. He can only say that he is not conforming to a convention. And if he finds it convenient not to conform to it, he can be given no good reason why he should not. (Honesty is not always the best policy in this universe of discourse.) He can only be *attacked* for not doing so. If "ought" is to be explained in terms of social pressures or hereditary influences, superstitious fears, then there will be a return to the jungle. Recent history emphasises that it will not be much use to rely on human feelings of benevolence. They are "natural" indeed—but they will not come naturally to us if we do not understand our own natures.

But could we not say that a moral demand speaks for itself and requires no religious interpretation? To the question "why ought we?" the answer would then be : "You must not ask that—we ought because we ought." I cannot think that this answer is likely to commend itself for very much longer. The nineteenth-century attempt to preserve the moral imperative while denying that it postulates a transcending of the finite is less plausible today than it was then. Appeals to "the spirit of man" or "the religion of humanity" are more obviously insufficient. If "ought" is not to indicate the summons of the transcendent Good, the "positivist" explanation will hold the field. It has always been a puzzle to me that some philosophers who are theists should ally themselves with positivists in so far as they regard "ought" as sufficiently intelligible without reference to the Absolute. I would venture to suggest to them that their suspicions of "the philosophy of value" are exaggerated. It is true that this approach has been adopted by very many thinkers whose views may be called in general "subjectivist" or "humanist" in a non-theistic sense. But it has also been adopted by very many thinkers, especially on the continent of Europe but frequently in the English-speaking countries, in the way in which I adopt it here. Unless appeals to experience are to be disallowed altogether, which would surely be fatal for any account of theism, there seems no good ground for maintaining this attitude of aloofness in regard to the moral evidence for God.

So, after this brief review of previous findings, it seems to me that if we accept the absolute, transcendent element in our experience, we shall be accepting at one and the same time the fact of human awareness, our contact with the infinite source, our state of tension towards it and our freedom to accept it or reject it as our goal; whereas, if we accept instead the relativist conclusion, we shall be turning our backs at one and the same time on respect for truth, on all objective values, on our moral aspirations and on that proper pride in our humanity which depends on the recognition of our spiritual freedom and destiny. Such blunt talk will offend polite ears. This is not theologising, it will be objected, still less philosophising, but sermonising. It does not matter what it is called. What matters is whether it can be plausibly denied.

But that is not at all to say that an unhesitating decision for the former of these alternatives can be claimed as of right from everyone. There are, I suppose, innumerable honest doubters, people who find the difficulties of accepting either alternative insuperable, and there are others who are, apparently, incapable of realising that such questions arise at all—they may be vaguely aware that some people think about them, but that they have any relevance to their own existences never occurs to them. A Christian must hold that it will have to occur sometime. As for the honest doubters, I have expressed the view that they have in fact embraced the "absolutist" alternative in so far as they regard the pursuit of truth as incumbent upon them. It remains that, even with the best will in the world, they may find themselves unable to advance. They cling to something—which, I have come to think, they would mostly agree to call *value*. But, they may say, any attempt to pin it down brings us up against impossibilities. It is that situation which must be further explored at this point.

In our society it is a situation in which the claims of theism and the claims of Christianity involve one another in a way which, I think, needs to be more clearly recognised. Theism might come to seem acceptable if the support which Christianity is supposed to give it were more impressive. If theism *were* true, Christianity *would* seem more impressive. In other words, we have to consider not only the difficulties which theism presents to the acceptance of Christianity but also the fact that theism is often thought to have had its best chance with Christianity and finally to have failed because Christianity has failed. And to say that Christianity is a bad advertisement for theism is not just to say that Christians have behaved so badly in the "ages of faith" and seem to behave nowa-days much like everyone else. The usual reply that without Chris-tianity things would have been still worse and that Christianity in any case has to be judged by its best is a fair enough answer to that, although unless Christianity's best can be exhibited here and now it will not be a very effective one. The burden of the com-plaint which I have in mind is that Christians, even when their behaviour is admirable, do not seem, by and large, to be *interested* in God. Can they therefore believe in him in a way which is any-thing more than a taking for granted?

There are indeed a great many books on the philosophy of religion produced in our time, and this does suggest a certain revival of interest. But academic debates in which the participants are so often non-theists (or so-called theists who reject the "trans-cendent element") are not much to the present point. And *that* is the impression given by practising Christians that they are not "in touch" with the God whom they claim to serve. In fact, I would say, they *are* "in touch" with him because they do serve him; in doing what they know to be their duty they may be very closely "in touch". But that applies to so many other people who make no religious professions. I am not suggesting that these prac-tising Christians are without Christian faith, but it would certainly appear that it is little developed and that they have little under-standing of it. They may have a fair amount of information *about* Christianity and may know the official answers to questions about God. They may come to church and say their prayers and do all the right things. There is no question about their taking religion seriously, and in that sense they are interested in it very much. But to be interested in *God* means something more. It is not just a matter of learning things *about* him. It presupposes some personal acquaintance with him which makes all the difference to the shape of one's mind and what I can only refer to as the tone and colour of one's thoughts and feelings. It is this, fundamentally, and not academic competence with which talk about "the educated Christian" should be concerned. What non-Christians look for and fail to find is that *newness* of life which Christians should possess. If they looked around more they would find it sooner or later. Monasteries, for example, if they are going concerns at all, are inhabited by people who are *interested* in God, and visitors to them come more and more for that reason. But there are not many monasteries.

These are the commonplaces of Christian preachers and apologists, but they have a peculiar relevance at the present time. To bring the present discussion to a point, how many Christians today *dwell on* their belief that they are destined to "eternal life"? Eternal life, unless we can consider it in the light of God (unless we are in some degree in "union" with him already), is surely most undesirable as well as most improbable. Christians are commonly adjured to face the possibility of hell. How many of them really face the possibility of heaven? Their attitude to death, for the most part, does not seem so very different from that of their non-Christian neighbours. It appears to me that at the present time this is a notably widespread phenomenon and a particularly significant indication of a widespread weakening of faith. But if something which I called "mysticism" is indeed meant for everyone, then something can be done about it.

Everyone who keeps his eyes open at all realises that "protesting" is not just a fashion which will die out in the usual way. It is true that many young people do not at all understand what they are protesting against. But behind all the confusion is a profound dissatisfaction which is certain to have immense consequences. What sort of consequences they are going to be will depend, eventually, upon whether Christianity is presented to them as the meaning of mysticism or as a mere moralism.

It may be said that one cannot expect everyone to be a metaphysician. But this is just what a Christian will have to expect if he expects Christianity to say anything to the world of the future. The alternative, so much favoured at present by religious writers, is to offer a God who suffers from our own limitations and is in some sort exposed to our own hazards. It is very clear to me that a policy of reducing Christianity's claims for God must make him seem unworthy of man's worship. An anthropomorphic God, in other words, is going to seem quite incredible. A Christian will have to be a metaphysician in so far as he will have to recognise, in the first place, that God is *different*; he will have to be positively aware of him *as* different. His "beyondness" must be apprehended in his immanence. Prayer as a deliberate attention to this "beyondness" will be indispensable.

God's mysteriousness must be stressed as much as his accessibility. I have not yet sufficiently stressed it. There is a certain agnosticism which is necessary when we are thinking about God. We must indeed say that all values are present in him if the relation in which the world stands to him is to be intelligible at all and if our inexpressible knowledge of him is to be "pointed to" at all, but when we speak of the convergence and fusion of values at infinity we have no more than an inkling of what this means. We have to bear in mind that in regard to the divine life itself we are largely ignorant.

It is particularly important to bear this in mind when we are considering the problem of evil. The honest doubter's most discussed difficulty is that things have gone wrong in the world which seem inexplicable on the theistic view, even if one accepts "the free will defence"; and I suggested that free will is not confined to ourselves, there being other intelligent creatures. But the more pressing difficulty, perhaps, is that the world as we see it does not seem to be a world in which God could be at work at all. If you stand in the middle of one of our great cities and ask yourself what is going on, doesn't it appear plainly that "God is dead"? The theologians who were saying that a few years ago are reported to have lost favour, but that is the affair of a minority. The average post-Christian has hardly heard of it or of "the God of the future", the developing God, who is being talked about now instead; for him God has always been an irrelevance. It is this pervasive attitude of mind which the honest doubter feels to be the normal and natural one in today's world. He has to be persuaded to think for himself. But even if he admits that one may have on occasion to go against the stream he may say that a God should make himself more obvious. And this is the point at which it must be emphasised that we cannot assess the limitations which a disordered world sets to the execution of God's super-generous designs. There must be no hesitancy in saying that these designs *are* infinitely generous, but we have to recognise that we do not *understand* this infinite generosity. It cannot contradict what we do understand by generosity. We cannot appeal to our ignorance if we are faced by plain contradictions. The truth which we know is God's truth. But when we are faced by obscurities we have to remember our ignorance, and in this sense we have to acknowledge that his ways may not be ours.

Here it may be remarked that, whereas theists seldom, if ever, deny that there is a problem of evil, their opponents seldom admit that, from their point of view, there is a problem of value or good, which, once faced, may seem much more recalcitrant. But it is not the opponents of theism with whom I am at present concerned but the post-Christian who is simply not interested one way or the other. There will not be much chance of interesting the typical product of late-twentieth-century education unless religious people adopt a new *style* of which, happily, we already see some beginnings. A style is the expression of an attitude of mind. The style to which I allude is the expression of what may be called, for short, the "absolutist" attitude of mind (which must be also a rational and a humanist one). What will be new about it is its greater awareness of the proper significance of theological ideas. Religious language will have to represent a more genuinely metaphysical outlook. There is a basic Christian metaphysic which I have tried to illustrate in this book. Current theology tends to jettison it with disastrous results. My contention is that we need to bring it up to date by accepting those implications of it which were not sufficiently recognised in earlier ages and which have to be faced if it is to recommend itself to the thought of our time.

I shall take some examples of what I have in mind. Religious people talk about God's "almighty power". The way in which they talk about it may show that they fail to realise how different his "power" is from what we ordinarily mean by the word : expenditure of energy, the means of imposing your will on people and the possession of unused resources. If you asked them whether God is extended in space, they would doubtless dismiss the notion as absurd. But they are unconsciously introducing the notion of quantity, and so of limitation, into their notion of his power. If they are not to appear ridiculous and if they themselves are not to give up God in the end, they will have to realise that God's "power" must mean the limitless energy which we apprehend in its enabling of all limited beings, starting with ourselves. It is not what we ordinarily mean by a "force". Although we are completely dependent upon it, it *offers* us our activities—it is for us to decide which we shall have. God's power is a *giving*; but he does not impose his gifts upon us. In other words, if God is to make sense at all, Christians will have to understand what is meant by "pure act" or "perfection" in traditional metaphysics, although they may not use its terminology. And their theologians will need to warn them on occasion of certain shortcomings in the traditional metaphysics, in particular the lingering anthropomorphism which pictures God as "choosing" as we choose and "needing" things as we need them.

Popular notions about providence provide another example. It is very often supposed that God so "overrules" the course of events that everything happens for the best; that is to say, the answer to the problem of evil is that the good which God wants can be attained only by "permitting" evil, moral and physical, on a vast scale. Apart from the question of what "permitting" can mean, this answer to the problem presents us with a God in whom nobody will be able to believe much longer. And it is combined somehow with the idea that God's attitudes can become more favourable to us as the result of petitionary prayer. It is going to become plain, I venture to say, that the notion of providence, if it is not to be altogether given up, must mean that God's attitude is always infinitely favourable to us and that in all circumstances we are given the opportunity of acting for the best—but if we are indeed morally free, then we cannot say that everything must happen for the best. That the possibility of spiritual failure is bound up with a credible God is the conclusion which must be squarely faced.

Dissatisfaction with time-honoured religious language is in itself a promising sign, but theologians, instead of taking the opportunities which this offers them, often merely echo it. This talk of God as a King, people say, and of the service which we owe him has no appeal for us. It is a relic of feudal times. God wants us to be his collaborators. What ought to be said about this is that God is always the giver and we are always the receivers. Unless that is understood as the necessary basis, theism will not seem acceptable to intelligent people. In that context, but only in that context, we can say that God serves us. To say that we serve him is to say that we are dependent upon him for everything and that his offer of himself to us and to all men is all that matters in the end.

So the alternatives presented to Christian theologians seem to me quite clear-cut. They can take up with a non-metaphysical God (sometimes called "the God of Revelation") who is at risk, limited and changeable, and this is the first stretch on a slippery slope which leads to secular humanism; or they can maintain the Christian faith in God's infinity and immutability, and in that case they will need to recognise, I think, that even traditional theologians have not been wholly consistent in this matter. Christianity without metaphysics is an absurdity. We might say that we want less metaphysics in the sense that we want fewer metaphysical entities. But we need more insistence on the fundamental metaphysics enshrined in the religious consciousness. This is where mysticism takes its rise, and to appreciate its true significance we must understand what the Christian mystics are trying to teach us.

APPENDIX I

PROFESSOR T. R. MILES ON RELIGIOUS EXPERIENCE

Of the series to which Professor Miles's *Religious Experience* belongs (New Studies in the Philosophy of Religion, Macmillan) the General Editor, Dr W. D. Hudson, says that its "general approach is from the standpoint of contemporary analytical philosophy". So one would not expect that it would be particularly favourable to religion unless perhaps an unusual sense is given to "religion". Professor Miles, who reveals himself as a Quaker, gives it such a sense : its importance, for him, lies in the holding of "certain 'cosmic' views, i.e. views about the nature and destiny of man". "Belief in a God", he explains, "is one answer to these cosmic questions" (p 18) and he is chiefly concerned to show that the grounds on which that belief is commonly based are without substance.

"I shall argue", he writes on his first page, "that it is a mistake to postulate special entities called 'religious experiences' if these are thought of as 'non-material' in character or as providing recondite information about a 'non-material world'." He goes on to attack the equation of "experiences" with "mental events", appealing to Wittgenstein and to Professor Gilbert Ryle in a way which is very familiar to some of us (he seems unaware of the many decisive criticisms of Ryle's *The Concept of Mind*). I can only repeat that the difference between a state of awareness and a state of unawareness is something which cannot sensibly be denied and that this entirely justifies our use of the contrasting terms "body" and "mind", indicative of a fundamentally important distinction without which it is impossible to understand ourselves (or, therefore, to apprehend God). Apart from the statement on p 41 that "the idea of a 'non-material Being' is foreign to all biblical thought", the most remarkable passage, perhaps, in this connection is concerned with what Miles calls "ontological differences". First he offers some "trivial examples" of them, one of which is : "in providing someone with a drink I might use a cup and reach out towards him, but it would be odd to say that I used both a cup and a reach . . .". He then proposes that "the word 'experience' is ontologically *dissimilar* from the word 'behaviour'; and, if this is right, it follows that arguments as to whether psychologists should or should not study experience *in addition to* behaviour are misguided" (p 24). As an attempt to argue "mental events" out of existence this seems to me peculiarly unconvincing.

In the same paragraph Miles observes : "Much popular thinking

Appendix I

assumes that one can ask whether there exists a God *in addition to* ordinary familiar objects." He is right to point out that one can properly ask questions about the "existence" of anything only in a particular context. If we are to say that *we* "exist", then we cannot say that *God* "exists" and mean the same thing by it. What he fails to recognise is that there is a claim to be *aware of God* which does not make him an item of the world's furniture but affirms him as inexpressible and "points to" him as the infinite source of existence. Miles seems to think that we are not entitled to claim any evidence for God as "objective" because there can be no appropriate criteria for deciding about it : "A buzzing in my head is different from a buzzing caused by a bee; the buzzing of the bee is 'objective' in the sense that both I and others can be aware by independent criteria, viz. sight and touch, of the presence of the bee . . ."; but if anyone wants to say that God is the "source" of a "religious experience", then "the onus is on him to give a meaning to those terms . . ." (p 30). First it must be repeated that there is a claim to an awareness of *God,* not of phenomena which are held to postulate God. But it is the demand for objective criteria which is of special interest. Does Miles believe that no valid claim can be made unless these criteria can be brought to bear on it? I could make a valid claim, in certain conditions, about a buzzing in my head, although I might not be able to *prove* it to the satisfaction of those around me. Equally a man could claim, without logical impropriety, to be aware of God, although this would not convince other people. And he could call this an "objective" experience, meaning that he claims to be aware of what is not a dream or a hallucination but a *presence.* But of course that word is only a "pointer", too.

Towards the end of the book (p 55) Miles speaks of "experiences which people throughout the ages have found to be of cosmic significance—the beauty of the sky and of flowers, the problems raised by death, and the sense of wonder at the glories of artistic creation". "I see no justification", he continues, "for saying that people's attitude to cosmic questions should not be influenced by experiences of this kind." And he is prepared to call such experiences "self-authenticating". After setting out the opening bars of the last movement of Beethoven's Fifth Symphony he says truly : "the music here speaks for itself : it is not 'evidence' for something else." So it is with the awareness of God. I wish Miles had told us in what ways and to what effect our "attitude to cosmic questions" is, in his view, legitimately influenced by such experiences. But he does end by telling us that "the demand in religion for commitment is unconditional" (p 59); his account of this is impressive, and I hope that he will pardon me for saying that it sounds rather like what I mean by "theism".

APPENDIX II

NELSON PIKE ON TIMELESSNESS

The difficulties which arise about God's timelessness have been discussed with much learning and logical acumen by Dr Nelson Pike (*God and Timelessness*, Routledge and Kegan Paul, 1970). "It is now my suspicion", he writes in conclusion, "that the doctrine of God's timelessness was introduced into Christian theology because Platonic thought was stylish at the time and because the doctrine appeared to have considerable advantage from the point of view of systematic elegance" (pp 189-90). It seems to me a doctrine which declares one of the findings of the developed religious consciousness or, more precisely, an aspect of what it finds, one which is left in the shade when there is little reflection going on or reflection of only a rather unsophisticated kind. I cannot conceive that there is much of a future for the notion of a God who is *in* time. To be *in* time is to have one's existence "scattered" or "spread out", not "all at once". I have put inverted commas round those expressions because they are not descriptions, in the normal sense of that word, but "pointers"—and the situation to which they point is one in which we recognise our existence as limited because timeful and by the same token recognise that "behind" it is its unlimited, timeless, source. "Timelessness", then, means that God is not "scattered" or "spread out". He is "all together" or one and undivided in a sense which is not true of ourselves. We need to grow. What we want to attain is union with a power which has no need to grow, because it has no needs of any kind —that is why it is pure generosity. Or again, a God who should be *in* time must be "going on" now and will be "going on" tomorrow and (I suppose) for ever. He will be ever incomplete. That is to contradict what religion in general and Christianity in particular *mean* by "God".

It is, of course, true, as Pike points out, that religious language, in particular the language of the bible, seems regularly to speak of God as having *duration*. This is because all language is of its nature time-conditioned; it cannot jump out of its own skin. But to say that God "endures forever" is a way of saying that he is always the same. And this "is" and this "always" have a non-temporal reference, despite the fact that they have also a temporal one. They have a temporal reference for the reason just mentioned, that language is itself temporal and cannot *describe* the non-temporal. But "is" and "always" *point to* it by denying that God has a past (that he *loses* anything) or a future (that he *gains* anything). What it amounts to is that, from the point of view of the reflective religious consciousness, the proposal that God is *in* time is "counter-intuitive", to use an expression which Pike uses on other occasions.

The "intuition" that God timelessly produces temporal objects is one which he cannot accept. I have maintained above that, although this is certainly not an *imaginable* state of affairs, it contains no internal contradiction. That Pike is not prepared to adopt this metaphysical approach is suggested at an early stage when he says of God's perfect goodness that it is "something which we have been given in revelation" (p 23), apparently excluding any *apprehension* of it, and when he goes on to discuss God's immutability as a matter of (alleged) *logical* (instead of metaphysical) necessity. And God is often referred to as "a particular individual". It is worth noting, in passing, that Pike does not seem to regard "timelessness" itself as meaningless because he concludes that it would be "an essential property of any individual possessing it" (p 28). But he finds no sufficient reason for concluding that God possesses it.

What, then, in his view, are the objections to that conclusion? Apart from the general difficulty of transcending time in our thought, they seem to be contained in certain passages of his final chapter. "God's timelessness", he writes, "does not square well with the standard Christian belief that God once assumed finite, human form . . . But, of course, it is generally acknowledged by Christian theologians that the God-man paradox *is* a paradox" (pp 172-3). It is recognised that God's timelessness, in traditional theology, goes with the denial that he has *fore*knowledge (for he *sees* the timeful timelessly), but this is held to be "not in accord with the standard Christian conception of God" (p 174); the most important ground for this conclusion I take to be that a changeless God could not be "responsive to the needs and desires of finite beings" (p 175). Again "God is described as a loving individual having purposes and plans that are worked out in the development of his creation" (p 175), and this too is considered incompatible with timelessness. I shall not repeat what I have said above, with such objections in mind, about creation, the Incarnation and God's "unchanging beneficence". But it is interesting to note that Pike goes on to suggest that "God cannot cease to be benevolent" might be understood to mean "God is strongly disposed (perhaps *irreversibly* disposed) to act with benevolence towards others", and thus to say that he cannot change in this respect would express *"material rather than logical impossibility"*. However, "this analysis is compatible with the idea that the individual that is God changes in some ways" (p 178).

APPENDIX III

J. GALOT ON THE INCARNATION

In *Nouvelle Revue Théologique* of March, 1971, an article entitled "Dynamisme de l'Incarnation" appeared by the well-known Jesuit theologian, J. Galot. I select it to illustrate the present tendency, even among traditional theologians, to reject the divine immutability or to make contradictory statements about it. This was discussed in some detail in my *The Absolute and the Atonement*. The article which I here discuss shows that this attitude of mind is shared even by a theologian who in the ordinary way is particularly firm in resisting mere "fashions" in theology and who would be generally regarded as a pillar of Roman orthodoxy.

Here he tells us : "It is the Word, and not only a human nature, which passes into a new state. In this state he does not only enrich himself with a human nature; he becomes man." How can a divine person enrich himself? And a little later we find : "But . . . this becoming implies a certain immutability in the Word . . . He remains identically the Word. . . ." Thus a "kenotic" theory according to which the Word loses divine status seems to be avoided. But something is *added* to the Word, so that there is a real change in *him*. It is a change of such a kind, Galot goes on to explain, that the Word "has had personally the experience of human life, of his own human life"; in fact, as he insists, the Word as such has undergone suffering and death. Again, is this thinkable of a divine person? It is, of course, true, as Galot points out, that passages in the New Testament seem to support such conclusions and that they have been, naturally, echoed down the ages. But they have also been rephrased down the ages by Christians of the more reflective kind in such a way as to make them thinkable (this was discussed in Chapter Five, above). The question is whether Christian theologians of our time are going to take up with an anti-metaphysical line of thought (cutting off, incidentally, all hope of *rapprochement* with non-Christian Orientals) or whether they are going to recognise that our theology has been, in the past, not *too* metaphysical but not consistently metaphysical.

Galot is not unaware of the difficulties of his position. After remarking that the "sending" of the Son, in which the Father and the Holy Spirit are "engaged", is "a novelty arising from an immutable divine being" he acknowledges that "it obliges us to seek a reconciliation of this novelty with the divine immutability." Indeed it does. But Galot can only echo Karl Rahner's formula, which has been repeated with approval by a number of other writers, that "the immutable in itself becomes mutable in another." Since that formula was produced, some ten years ago, I have been making unsuccessful attempts to discover what it may mean. Galot thinks to recommend his point of view by urging that the freedom of God carries with it a "gratuitous superabundance of vitality", a "dynamism". This sounds vaguely exciting; in fact it is the beginning of an anthropomorphic account of the divine life. For we now read : "The aspect of novelty results again from the fact that the decision of the Incarnation was taken by the Father in response to the sin of humanity. It shows how the Father was affected by this sin. . . ." We also read that "the act of love which commands the Incarnation emanates from God himself : it is not implied in the divine nature, since, in regard to this nature, it is freely accomplished and has a fundamental character of gratuitousness, of non-necessity." If theology is not to be written off as mythical, such pictures of God must be given up. In this book I have tried to suggest how they can be given up.

APPENDIX IV

WALTER HILTON AS THEOLOGIAN

To end this book, I give some illustration of the sort of writing to which I have referred as that of the classical mystical tradition. The passages printed below are taken from the second book of Walter Hilton's *The Scale of Perfection*. Hilton was an Augustinian Canon who died at the Priory of Thurgarton, Nottinghamshire, in 1396. He was writing during the Great Schism and in the middle of the Hundred Years' War, at a time when it must have seemed that everything was being turned upside down (Wat Tyler captured London in 1381, and the Lollards looked like being the Church of the future).

'He [God] openeth the inner eye of the soul when he lighteneth the reason through touching and shining of his blessed light, to see him and know him; not all fully at once, but little and little by divers times as the soul may suffer him. He seeth him not what he is, for that may no creature do . . . But he seeth him that he is an unchangeable being, sovereign might, sovereign soothfastness, sovereign goodness, a blessed life, an endless bliss . . ." (Chapter 32).

"It is commonly said that a soul shall see our Lord within all things and within itself. Sooth it is that our Lord is within all creatures, but not on that manner as a kernel is hid within the shell of a nut, or as a little bodily thing is holden within another mickle. But he is within all creatures as holding and keeping them in their own being, through subtlety and might of his own blessed kind and cleanness unseeable. For right as a thing which is most precious and most clean is laid innermost, right so by that likeness it is said that the kind of God, that is most precious, most clean and most ghostly, furthest from bodilihood, is hid within all things . . . Also it is said in Holy Writ that *God is light*. So saith Saint John. This light shall not be understood as for bodily light, but it is understood thus, that God is truth and soothfastness, for soothfastness is ghostly light. Then he that most graciously knoweth soothfastness, best seeth God. And nevertheless it is likened to the bodily light for this reason. Right as the sun to the bodily eye showeth itself and all bodily things by it : right so soothfastness, that is God, showeth to the reason of the soul itself first, and by itself all other ghostly things that needeth to be known of a soul" (Chapter 33).

"We do right naught but suffer him and assent to him; for that is the most that we do, that we assent wilfully to his gracious working in us. And yet is that will not of us, but of his making, so that methinks that he doth in us all that is well done, and yet we see it not. And not only doth he thus, but after this love doth more. For he openeth the eye of the soul and showeth to the soul the sight of Jesus wonderfully, and the knowing of him, as the soul may suffer it thus by little and by little; and by that sight he ravisheth all the affection of the soul to him" (Chapter 34).

"That manner of meat that least letteth and least troubleth the heart, and may keep the body in strength—be it flesh, be it fish, be it but bread and ale—that I trow the soul chooseth to have, if it may come thereby. For all the business of the soul is to think on Jesus with reverent love ever, without letting of anything, if it might. And therefore, since it must needs somewhat be letted and hindered, the less it is letted and hindered by meat and drink or any other thing the liefer it is" (Chapter 39).

"But then might thou say thus : that we should live only in troth and not covet ghostly feelings nor regard them if they come. For the apostle saith : *The righteous man liveth in troth*. Unto this I say that bodily feelings, be they never so comfortable, we shall not covet, nor regard them much if they come. But ghostly feelings such as I speak of, if they come in the manner that I have said before, we should ever desire . . . We should covet to feel ever the lively inspiration of grace made by the ghostly presence of Jesus in our soul, if we might; and to have him in our sight with reverence, and ever feel the sweetness of his love by a wonderful homeliness of his presence" (Chapter 41).

DATE DUE

JAN 0 8 '91		
JUN 2 8 '91		